Zzyzx: History of an Oasis

San Bernardino County, California

Anne Q. Duffield-Stoll

California Desert Studies Consortium
The California State University

Santa Susana Press
University Library
California State University, Northridge

ISBN 937048-49-6
Copyright 1994. California Desert Studies Consortium,
California State University, Fullerton.
Desert Studies Contributed Series Number 65

Contents

Acknowledgements

Although it feels like another lifetime ago, there was a time when driving in on Zzyzx Road on a Friday night was a new, slightly anxious experience for me, before I got my own 4WD. I was still 100% city girl then, going to graduate school, taking a field class at the Desert Studies Center. At that time the first part of Zzyzx Road from the freeway was soft, deep gravel and I would try to hit that stretch with some fortitude, to "keep my speed up" like they told me. The road pebbles would rattle around inside the wheel wells of my little Honda and fly out like a spray of bullets as I went careening along, hitting every dip. Then came the part they called "wash board." This was the beginning of my desert education at Zzyzx.

Now driving in on Zzyzx Road means greeting an old friend, and the lessons continue. My tutors are many and I owe them all my profound gratitude for opening their resources to me, and for opening me to the desert.

I wish to gratefully acknowledge the support of the Desert Studies Consortium, of the two Directors who made this book happen; first, Gerald Scherba, who envisioned the project and commissioned the manuscript, and second, Bill Presch, who followed through and brought it to publication. To the folks at the DSC, Alan, Rob, Dawn, Josh, Tim and Norma, I owe a heart-felt thanks for your support and friendship over the years.

There are three more very important people to be gratefully acknowledged for their help with this booklet: Dennis G. Casebier, Arda M. Haenszel, and Germaine Moon. All three have always generously shared with me and it has been my great good fortune to have been individually mentored by them, the undisputed top experts on East Mojave Desert history. I can only hope they feel this booklet is at least a partial repayment for their investment.

CHAPTER ONE

Introduction and Prehistory

This is the story of a very special place, an oasis in the desert known historically as Soda Springs, which many today call Zzyzx. As with any oasis, the powerful appeal of this place is the water, flowing sparkling clear and abundant. Water means life on the desert, relief from burning thirst. It means a cool drink at a shaded pool, a haven on a scorching hot day. Soda Springs is a desert oasis in this classic sense, perched on the western rim of Soda Dry Lake playa in the East Mojave Desert of San Bernardino County, California. Looking south from the highway community of Baker on Interstate 15, the oasis of Soda Springs is just visible at the base of the Soda Mountains, a small patch of green against a stark, dry landscape of white, grey and brown.

In the desert, appearances are deceiving. Soda Springs seems remote, isolated from traffic and the flow of human events, a lonely outpost. In fact, it has been an important watering hole for travelers for hundreds if not thousands of years. Those who know the East Mojave know Soda Springs, though they may call it something else, such as "Fort Soda" or "Zzyzx" (Zzyzx is pronounced "Zye-Zix"). By any other name, the water is still as wet and welcome.

Though many have passed through, few have lingered long at this oasis. A woman of the Chemehuevi Indian tribe is the only one known for certain to take her eternal rest here. Her people probably knew the place best, having stopped at the water for centuries on their seasonal journeys through the desert. In the modern reconstruction, the Chemehuevis are pictured traveling the desert in small family groups in tune with the seasonal changes. At a place like Soda Springs, they may have surprised and trapped small game that came to drink. At the water they bathed and filled their gourd jugs. In the shelter of the

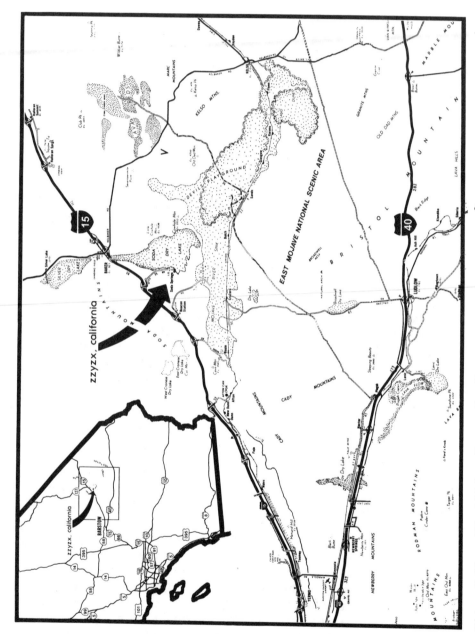

Figure 2. Map of East Mojave Desert, San Bernardino County, California.

limestone cliff they chipped stone tools and cooked a meal. They harvested the pods of honey and screw-bean mesquite, and maybe gathered the leaves from some of the lush, salt-tolerant plants on the east side of the spring. The Spanish called these plants "Yerba Mansa" (*Anemopsis californica*) and said the leaves had medicinal properties [72].

Perhaps the ancestors of the Chemehuevis and Mohaves, the most recent native desert-dwellers, knew stories of Older Ones who came before, when fresh water filled the ancient lakes and large game animals were plentiful. Today the tools of these early hunters are found in quarries high up on the Soda Mountains and on the sandbars along the once-marshy borders of ancient Lake Mojave.

The Chemehuevi woman may also have known of the white men, the soldiers and teamsters and prospectors who came later, who followed the roads through the desert and found Soda Springs. They came for the water too, though it tasted bitter and sometimes the mules wouldn't drink it. But what the water lacked in taste, it made up for in clarity and abundance. When Mojave Road travelers between Prescott and San Bernardino arrived hot and dusty at the springs, they were greeted by a special treat. A rock-lined pool, constantly refilled by flowing water, awaited them for that greatest of luxuries, a bath.

Water, too, attracted later developers to Soda Springs; water to mix with crushed ore in an arastre, water to fill evaporating ponds to recover the salts, water to cure the ills of modern society by soaking and cleansing, inside and out. A belief in the power of mineral water to restore health and well-being brought many hopefuls to this desert oasis when it was first given the name Zzyzx Mineral Springs in 1944. Today the water is still a magnet to those who visit and use the Desert Studies Center's teaching and research facilities. College students who come to study the geology, anthropology, flora and fauna at the water's edge have replaced resort guests. The oasis still makes this spot unique.

Prehistory

Human history in this part of the East Mojave goes back as far as it goes anywhere in California. Evidence of very early occupation in the Soda Springs area comes from solidly-dated stone artifacts found in association with Carbon 14-dated shells of the freshwater clam *Anodonta* at Silver Dry Lake playa (north of Baker, once part of Pleistocene Lake Mojave). Warren and Ore (1978) found three stone graver tools (perhaps used for perforation) and the broken base of a projectile point there in a stratum which they dated to 10,270 years ago (+/−160 years, Y-2406). They also dated surface material from the shores of Silver Dry Lake to about 8000 years ago [71].

This research indicates that early hunter-gatherers camped near Soda Springs during at least two periods in the past when water filled the dry playa of Pleistocene Lake Mojave. When full, this shallow body of water covered both modern Silver Dry Lake and Soda Dry Lake playas. Lake Mojave's shoreline must have made a very inviting prehistoric destination. Primarily the product of distant run-off, Lake Mojave existed from approximately 22,000 years ago to 8,700 years ago, with ephemeral episodes when water again briefly filled the basin repeating into recent times. This estimate is based upon the radiocarbon dating of shell, tufa and organic matter from Silver Dry Lake cores and shore features [21].

From these distant beginnings, the water at Soda Springs has continued to attract visitors to the present day. The full spectrum of human use of the desert is revealed at this oasis, which makes this place especially important to those who study human adaptation to desert environments through time. For a summary of previous and on-going archaeological research at Soda Springs and environs, see Appendix I. For an outline of the cultural sequence for this part of the Mojave Desert, see Appendix II.

Proto-History: Mohaves and Chemehuevis

The Mohave Indians living along the Colorado River and the Chemehuevi and other desert tribes inhabiting the interior were doubtless familiar with the oasis we call Soda Springs. The Mohaves regularly traveled west across the desert up the Mojave River and over the San Bernardino Mountains to trade with coastal Indians as far away as Santa Barbara [58]. Large and well-built physically, Mohave runners could make the trip to the coast in just a few days [14].

Though as travelers and traders they ranged the desert, the Mohaves' homeland was well-defined. Because they relied on flood-plain agriculture for their subsistence, the Mohave villages were located within the narrow strip along the banks of the Colorado River. Their traditional territory extended on both sides of the river beginning at its emergence from the Grand Canyon southward and reaching as far south as modern-day Parker, Arizona.

The Mohaves were first encountered by Spanish explorers, perhaps as early as 1540 with the expedition of Hernando de

Alarcon. Spanish Captain Melchior Diaz and Juan de Onate may also have had contact with these river people during their separate travels along the Colorado, though their descriptions are somewhat ambiguous [58]. Today there are nearly 400 Mohaves living on the 38,000-acre Fort Mojave Reservation near Needles, California [23].

Soda Springs also falls within traditional range of the Chemehuevi Indians (the Vanyume, a tribe related to the Serrano, may also have used the oasis [36], though their presence there has not been confirmed archaeologically). The Chemehuevis, also known as Southern Paiutes, speak a Numic dialect of the Uto-Aztecan language, are relatively small in stature, and in prehistoric times did not practice agriculture. They lived in the classic style of desert hunter-gatherers, in small family groups, using the food and shelter the desert provided them. Although they sometimes baked pots, the Chemehuevis are famous for their high-quality twined baskets. A network of trails crossed through their territory over which the Chemehuevis hunted and traded with tribes living along the Colorado and as far west as the coast.

Within the proto-historic period (1600 A.D.–1850), a portion of the Chemehuevi tribe settled on the Colorado River near Cottonwood Island as neighbors of the Mohaves and adopted many Mohave ways. Other Chemehuevi people remained in the desert at oases such as Twentynine Palms, where they eventually joined the reservation system and experienced some blending with Cahuilla and Serrano Indians [41].

The "Contact Period" or era of transition, which began when Europeans arrived in the New World and which ended so painfully elsewhere in California, seems to have passed relatively easily at Soda Springs. Who can be sure just when the ripple-effect of this world-shattering encounter first reached this desert water hole? No written records provide that information. If the few panels of petroglyphs near Soda Springs record that event—or any event, for that matter—they have yet to be deciphered. As elsewhere, European goods and diseases traveled through the native community well ahead of the soldiers and settlers themselves.

The earliest explorers to cross the Mojave Desert did not stop at Soda Springs. If we correctly understand the historic descriptions, the early travelers trekked straight across the southern end of Soda Lake over soft and sandy ground, often in some discomfort for lack of water. Were the Mohave guides literally taking the shortest distance between water holes, as no doubt instructed, or were they avoiding Soda Springs for some reason?

CHAPTER TWO

Spaniard and Mexican Explorers
1776 to 1829

The first European to venture across the Mojave Desert did so with Mohave Indian guides (Note: by modern convention, the fort, the desert and the river are spelled with a "j"; the Indian tribe and the county in Arizona are spelled with an "h"). The route the Indians chose was reputedly long-established by this time. The first certain written description of the area near Soda Springs comes from the diary of the intrepid padre, Fr. Francisco Garcés.

Leaving Arizona in 1775 as a member of Juan Bautista de Anza's second expedition to southern California, Garcés parted company with Anza at Yuma and continued north up the Colorado into Mohave territory. On February 28, 1776 Garcés was welcomed at a large Mohave village near present-day Needles which he named "San Pedro de los Jamajabs" (pronounced "hama-ha-beys"). Garcés is believed to be the first white man to enter the Mohave homeland and later the first to "set foot upon the shores of the Mojave River" [48].

While staying with the Mohaves, Garcés learned of their far-ranging trading expeditions. He expressed a desire to travel to the coast and his hosts offered to show him the way. In his journal entries, Garcés briefly described the unnamed landforms he saw during his historic "entrada" across the Mojave Desert. There have been two important translations of Garcés' diary [19, 29] and many subsequent reassessments [for example, 8, 64, 70]. Based on an analysis of the journal and his own intimate knowledge of the desert, author Dix Van Dyke argued persuasively that Garcés visited the Providence Mountains and Devil's Playground via Foshay Pass on his way west (64). Perhaps the most easily recognized topographic feature described by Garcés is "El Arroyo de Los Martires" which he reached on

March 9, 1776. This is clearly the mouth of modern Afton Canyon at the sink of the Mojave River, some fifteen miles southwest of Soda Springs.

There is also no mistaking Garcés' description of the Mojave River itself which he called "El Rio de Los Martires." Working backward (eastward) from March 9, on the previous day Garcés had been six leagues northeast of the Sink of the Mojave (1 league = roughly 2.6 miles) at a place he called "Los Pozos de San Juan de Dios." This March 8 camp he described as "some very copious water holes . . . There is quite a lot of grass available. This is where the Vanyume nation starts" [70]. Could Garcés have been describing the oasis at Soda Springs? It is possible, though there are other viable candidates (for example, the waterholes used later by Fr. Nuez and Jedediah Smith along the southern border of Soda Lake). Unfortunately the Spaniard gave no other clues as to the location of "Los Pozos."

After their initial exposure to peace-loving, compassionate Fr. Garcés, the native impression of Anglo-Europeans could only have deteriorated. Being tied to their riverbank fields, the Mohaves suffered great cultural disruption from Spanish exploration of the Colorado, as did their neighbors to the south around Yuma, the Quechan Indians. As a result, the Mohaves' respect for the Spanish concept of property rights declined dramatically and their reception for travelers crossing the river became decidedly less cordial.

For the next twenty years, the Spanish attempted to protect their colonization efforts and trade routes with a show of force against the Indians but they were poorly equipped and greatly outnumbered. From the Spanish point of view, as Walker points out,

> Within the first three years of colonization, it became evident that the vast interior of California—the Colorado Desert, the Mojave Desert, and the San Joaquin Valley—was a liability rather than an asset. All three of these areas became havens and escape routes for runaway mission Indians, deserting soldiers, and marauding Indians who, for various reasons, substituted their ancient trade for illicit and lucrative endeavors [70].

Typically, Spanish (and later Mexican) settlers on the coast in southern California viewed the desert beyond the San Gabriel and San Bernardino Mountains as intimidating, a waterless wasteland filled with serious threats to men and beasts. (We know some modern Californians who also feel this way.) Thus knowledge of the Mojave Desert and the people dwelling in it languished at the level of ignorant conjecture through the 18th and into the 19th century.

A major source of friction with the Mohaves was the disruption of their ancient trading pattern with coastal tribes, now mostly made neophytes within the mission system. In 1816, warnings were sent out by Spanish officials to watch for Colorado Indians seeking to trade blankets and other goods. Such trade was prohibited and the Indians were to be punished if they returned (possibly because they represented unwanted competition for mission products) [26]. By 1819, trouble with Colorado River Indians (apparently with both the Mohaves and the Quechan) escalated to the point of being a serious threat to Spanish settlements.

Thus some 43 years after Garcés, another Spaniard ventured into the desert out of military necessity. "Murderous Mohave savages" were suspected of stealing horses and cattle in collusion with renegade San Gabriel Mission Indians. In September of 1819, Governor Pablo Vincente Sola decided to send three punitive expeditions to Mohave territory to make them "feel the arm of the government." Lieutenant Gabriel Moraga's company from Santa Barbara was one of those chosen.

An account of Moraga's desert trek is preserved in the diary of Fr. Joaquin Pasqual Nuez, minister of San Gabriel and chaplain of the expedition. Translated by George Beattie, the Nuez diary includes invaluable information about Indian settlement along the Mojave River. However, there is generally insufficient description of topographic features to be certain of the exact location of the Spanish camps [2].

Using Beattie's translation and an understanding of the terrain, Nuez' itinerary can be estimated. After crossing the San Bernardino Mountains, Lt. Moraga and company picked up the Mojave River near the Indian rancheria of "Guadalupe de Guapiabit" and followed it east [24]. Nuez renamed the flowing water "Rio de Las Animas" (the River of Blessed Souls). By December 1, 1819, Moraga's party had probably arrived at the Cady Ranch area on the river east of Barstow. The following day, Nuez reached the eastern-most point of his journey after crossing "a land very heavy (for travel) and alkaline . . . sixteen animals gave out on the road" [70]. This certainly could describe terrain near the Sink of the Mojave. Nuez gave the name "San Joaquin y Santa Ana de Angayaba" to his camp, and he and part of the party remained there while Lt. Moraga continued east [24]. A. L. Kroeber identified "Angayaba" as a Chemehuevi word, thus indicating that this camp was within Chemehuevi Indian territory [39].

Figure 3. Vicki Lane Hill rendition of Pool House, Zzyzx Mineral Springs.

Lt. Moraga and a portion of the company traveled east for another day and a half before his horses and provisions were exhausted and he was forced to turn back to rejoin Nuez. The journal provides the Indian (presumably Chemehuevi) names for Moraga's two camps, "Asamabeat" and "Guanachique," and it is possible that one of these refers to Soda Springs. The description of Guanachique also fits the water holes to the south and east of Soda Lake, however; "In Guanachique the explorers now concede . . . that by performing some labor a sufficient supply of water for the animals can be secured, for which purpose some tanks, wide and sufficiently deep should be dug in the earth **which is pure sand**" (emphasis added) [2]. In any event, Lt. Moraga never caught up with the Mohaves, who went unpunished by this Spanish expedition.

CHAPTER THREE

The First Americans
1829 to 1859

To date, no journals or diaries have been discovered which document expeditions or crossings of the Mojave Desert between the years 1819 and 1826. It appears that for these seven years, the desert-dwellers were allowed a breather of sorts before the next invasion hit. The words of American trapper and trader, Jedediah Strong Smith, provide the next glimpse of the Soda Springs area. Smith and party crossed to the south of Soda Springs, stopping at some brackish water holes (perhaps Guanachique?) where they found grass. Smith recorded his impressions of Soda Lake in his journal and in his correspondence, thus being the first American to do so.

In a letter to General William Clark, Superintendent of Indian Affairs, dated July 12, 1827, Smith told of following the "Seedskeeder" (the Colorado River) to the valley of the "Ammuchabas" (Mohaves) where he rested for fifteen days. After a false start during which he lost the trail, Smith returned to the village and contracted for Mohave guides [5]. Smith and his party entered the desert on horseback at a point on the Colorado opposite what was to become the site of Fort Mojave north of Needles. Sixteen days after his departure on November 10, 1826, Smith reached the Mission San Gabriel, thus becoming the first American to enter California overland [14].

> I travelled a west course fifteen days over a country of complete barrens, generally travelling from morning until night without water. I crossed a Salt plain about 20 miles long and 8 wide [Soda Lake]; on the surface was a crust of beautiful white salt, quite thin;—Under the surface is a layer of salt from a half to one & a half inches in depth;—between this and the upper layer there is about four inches of yellowish sand [44].

The Spanish authorities were less than delighted by Smith's arrival in California through "the back door," over the San Bernardino Mountains. Although well-treated by the padres, the party was detained and Smith was ordered to report to the governor in San Diego for questioning. After some weeks' delay, Smith and his men were allowed to leave.

In 1827, Jedediah Smith again entered Mohave Indian territory, not knowing that a few months before, several natives had been killed in skirmishes with trapper Ewing Young's group. An account of this incident has been preserved in the diary of James Ohio Pattie [25]. The Mohaves appeared to welcome Jedediah, who stayed with them three days, trading and resting his animals. Then on August 18, as part of Smith's party was on rafts fording the Colorado River and the rest waited on the bank to cross, the Mohaves attacked, killing ten men and taking the two women prisoner. Smith and eight other survivors were forced to flee into the desert on foot without water and with only Jedediah's memory of the route from the year before to guide them [14].

They traveled at night and Smith lost the trail, after which they very nearly died from thirst before finding a small spring. Shortly thereafter Jedediah climbed a peak and sighted the Salt Plain (Soda Lake) and recognized the path. "After dark we proceeded on across the Salt Plain and stopped at the holes I had dug when I passed before and there remained for the rest of the night" [44]. The next day Smith and his men reached the Mojave River where they were able to buy horses and canteens to continue their journey.

Jedediah Smith's experience with the Mohaves sent a warning to all who planned to cross at their village that travelers could no longer count on a warm welcome at the river. The massacre of over half of Smith's party was considered "one of the worst disasters in the history of the American fur trade" [14].

In the winter of 1829, an attempt was made to find a direct route across the desert from New Mexico to the California coast which avoided the Mohave villages. Under the leadership of Antonio Armijo, a trader from Santa Fe, New Mexico, a route was scouted which crossed the Colorado well to the north. Armijo's pioneering journey has earned him a place in history as "the first European known to have passed over the hostile desert between the Colorado River near Las Vegas and the Amargosa River, on to the Mojave River and [over] the Cajon Pass" [72].

Armijo's exact route west after crossing the Colorado is the subject of scholarly debate. Many believe this early caravan more or less blazed what was to become known as the Old

Spanish Trail [31]. An alternate interpretation suggests that instead of continuing west to Agua de Tomaso or Bitter Springs, now within the U.S. Army's Fort Irwin, Armijo may have turned southwest at what was labeled in his journal as "the lake of the miracle." This feature has been identified by Elizabeth von Till Warren as normally dry Silver Lake playa (perhaps with water in it). From there, Armijo may have proceeded around Soda Lake.

> It is very likely that Armijo chose to follow the borders of this [Soda] lake seeking springs or more important possible water sources that would cause the wet and muddy surface of this lake. It is a natural path, leading up the drainage channel into Soda Lake from Silver Lake, and would lead Armijo to several spring areas at the south end of Soda Lake, about a day's journey from his camp by the "lake of the miracle". Armijo's diary tells us that one day's journey from that lake, he camped at the "little spring of the badlands" [72].

Was this "little spring of the badlands" at Soda Springs, as Warren suggests? Possibly so, though other researchers have identified it as Bitter Springs. Again, there appears to be insufficient information to be certain.

After his successful crossing, a modification of Armijo's northern route became known as a viable alternative for trade caravans. This Old Spanish Trail and Garces' southern route through the Mojave Desert (known in time as the Mojave Trail) joined at the Mojave River west of Soda Springs at a place known historically as "Fork of the Roads" east of modern-day Yermo.

Relations with the Mohaves remained tense through the 1830s, though no further massacres were reported. Several parties crossed the Colorado through Mohave territory without mishap, unfortunately also without leaving descriptions of their water stops. Predictably, as Anglo-European travel across the desert increased, disruption of native American lifeways was also accelerated. For the few Indians who were armed and mounted, the response was to attempt a retaliatory raid. The huge herds of cattle and horses in the sparsely-settled San Bernardino Valley made an irresistable target. Horse raids reached epidemic proportions in the 1840s [68]. Unchecked by the authorities, these blatant acts further undermined Mexican control in California, already in terminal decline. The desert border of the San Bernardino Valley could not be secured and the floodgates of change were opened.

The Next Americans: Surveyors

Soda Springs apparently escaped attention during the tumultuous 1840s. California's historians and journalists clearly had their hands full documenting the effects of Indian raids, the Mexican-American War and the discovery of gold on the American River to focus on such a remote water hole. It seems the nation needed a few years to digest the momentous news from the western frontier before beginning to explore its new acquisition.

When it was admitted to the Union on September 9, 1850, the southern part of the new state of California was truly "terra incognita." The maps of the day showed the southern third of California as a large blank space, apart from the coastal strip. Information was urgently needed and a period of private and government-funded exploration began. One of the first government surveys to cross the Mojave Desert, led by Lt. Robert S. Williamson, stopped at Soda Springs [75].

Headed east toward the Colorado in November of 1853, Williamson and his men easily followed the trail along the Mojave River through what is now called Afton Canyon. The difficult moment arrived, as it had for Moraga some 35 years before, when the party reached the Sink of the Mojave.

> Upon emerging from the Cañon, we entered a sandy plain, and at once lost all signs of the river-bed. After travelling 13 miles across this plain, we were fortunate enough to find a hole containing water, and here we made our camp late at night. The water was barely sufficient for our nearly exhausted animals, and a long time was occupied in giving them a scanty supply . . .
>
> We observed to-day that to the north of our camp was a large lake-bed, and here we inferred the waters of the Mohave were collected. The question now was, whether this lake had an outlet, or whether it was a basin, and terminus of the Mohave. To ascertain this point, Lieutenant Stoneman and myself started to examine the lake, which was about fifteen miles long, and covered with an incrustation of salt, exceedingly bitter . . .
>
> We had found at the base of the hills, on the edge of the salt lake, several fine springs, slightly brackish but not unpalatable. Around these was good grass. The camp moved here, and the animals were refreshed by once more having as much to eat as they wanted [75].

This journal entry, dated November 15, 1853, is the first known written description of the springs on the edge of the Salt Lake (Soda Springs). After resting briefly, Williamson and party continued north to a second dry lake bed (Silver Lake) after which they picked up the Old Spanish Trail. This they followed west to Agua de Tomaso (Bitter Springs) and the Mojave River.

Williamson's explorations around "the Salt Lake" (it was not yet formally known as Soda lake) provided key information about the area, though it was not appreciated at the time. For example, Williamson and party discovered that Sink of the Mojave was just that, the last of those waters above ground. This settled the question of whether or not the Mojave River flowed into the Colorado, as some had theorized.

The next surveyor through the Mojave did not know of Williamson's discoveries, nor did he linger in the area to make any of his own. Lt. Amiel Weeks Whipple and party crossed the Mojave Desert westbound some four months after Williamson in March, 1854 [74]. Whipple's party was led by Mohave guides who again used the route across the southern end of Soda Lake. No one reported seeing Soda Springs, but from the diary of artist Heinrich Baldwin Mollhausen comes the origin of the name "Soda Lake".

> As we passed the volcanic hills and sand downs, we saw here and there fine blades of grass sprouting out of the ground, and were induced, for the sake of our cattle, to make a short halt. From this point we had a view over the second half of the sandy valley, and it looked like a field of snow.
>
> At first we supposed this white appearance to be some delusive atmospheric effect, but we soon found that we were on the bank of the spacious bed of a lake from which every drop of water had been dried up; but the salt with which the water had been impregnated had been deposited in a crust half an inch thick upon the loose earth, into which we broke to the ankles, so that a deep path was formed as we walked or rode after one another.
>
> Through this white plain, *which we named Soda Lake* [emphasis added] we proceeded in a south-westerly direction . . . [42].

The surveys of 1853–1854 provided much new scientific information about California's mountains, deserts and waterways, but failed in their original mission, which was to settle the question of the "best" route for a proposed Pacific Railroad. As several routes appeared feasible, the decision became more a question of politics than topography, and so the matter was sent back to the smoke-filled rooms of Washington D.C. for a time.

At the end of the 1850s, new key players entered Mojave Desert history; southern California-bound emigrants. Many were drawn to the Mojave by reports of a new wagon route across the desert laid out by Edward F. Beale in 1857. These desert travelers were a different breed; not wily mountainmen or surveyors on horseback but farmers and freighters with ox teams and loaded wagons. They hoped for a clear track to the coast with reliable water and feed and no surprises, but in the Mojave this was a far cry from what they got.

Beale's route led across the desert via the Mohave villages. Resting and resupplying at that point on the Colorado before the last dry stretch made the trip easier and safer, as long as the Mohaves remained cooperative. In the 1850s, however, the reception at the river was, if anything, even more hostile than before. The situation exploded into violence on August 30, 1858 when a group of emigrants camped at the Colorado was attacked by Mohaves. At least twenty emigrants were wounded and one was killed, and in a separate ambush, an entire family of seven was massacred [63]. The results were decisive for the Mohaves and for the future of the Mojave wagon road.

> . . . Back at the Mohave Villages, the Indians probably felt they had successfully defended their homeland. The native mind could not have comprehended the power of the white man and the determination with which he would protect and avenge depredations conducted against his kind. The only thing the Mohaves had accomplished was to hasten the day of their own destruction . . . Within a year hundreds of soldiers would come to their land, a fort would be established in their midst, and many Mohaves would be killed [14].

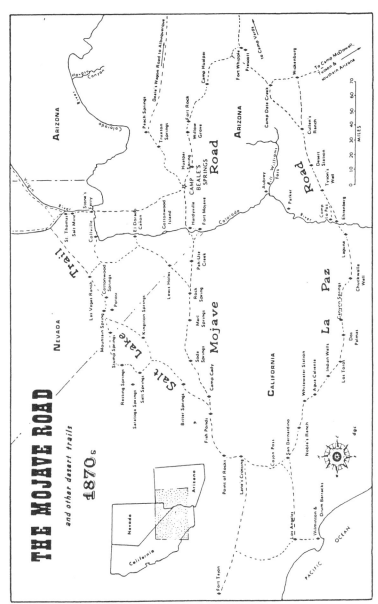

Figure 4. The Mojave Road and other desert Trails of the East Mojave Desert in the 1870s. Courtesy of Dennis Casebier.

CHAPTER FOUR

The Wagon Years
1859 to 1904

U.S. Army at Soda Springs

General Newman Clarke in San Francisco responded quickly to the news of the massacre at the Colorado by sending a large force under the command of Major William Hoffman to subdue the Mohaves, once and for all. Mission accomplished, in April, 1859 Hoffman established a permanent post, known as Fort Mojave, at the place where Beale's wagon road crossed the river north of present-day Needles.

Support and supplies for the new army post were urgently needed from the beginning. When flat-bottomed riverboats steaming up the river from Yuma proved unequal to the task, the clear alternative was to run supply wagons overland from Los Angeles. This meant new expeditions to check the feasibility of the route for military and commercial freight wagons. Several itineraries published in the Los Angeles newspapers during this period mentioned Soda Springs. The following is typical:

> May 14, 1859: Soda Springs. 33 miles—abundant supply of water. Rough road and sandy. This is the roughest part of the whole route. A steep hill; only two hills on the road. Heavy sand between Marl and Soda springs.
>
> On the other side of Soda Lake, bunch grass tolerable plenty. The Lake is dry, alkali two or three inches deep, five miles across, and at least 15 miles long [Los Angeles *Star* in 15].

Captain Winfield Scott Hancock was handed the assignment of supplying Fort Mojave from the quartermaster's headquarters in Los Angeles. On October 21, 1859, Hancock sent the first full wagon train to the Colorado by way of the Mojave

Trail (now called the Mojave Road). There were ten wagons in the train pulled by eight mules each. The itinerary recorded by teamster Joseph Winston on the eastbound trip indicates his party visited Soda Springs.

> Oct. 31, kept on down the river through a gorge [the present Afton Canyon], the mountains rising on both sides from two to four hundred feet on perpendicular clifts. The pass is two to three hundred yards wide and four miles long. Coming out of the gorge the road enters upon a large plain of coarse sand, with some dwarf grease wood. Here the Mojave river sinks. Its waters however, find their way over the plain in time of floods to Soda Lake where we are camped at 4 P.M., 19 miles. Course about N.E., road sandy.
>
> At this place there are some five or six acres of rushes and salt grass about the springs, which furnish a large supply of water. There is also plenty of galeta [grass] grown near this place [Los Angeles *Southern Vineyard* in 14].

This first wagon train reached the Colorado without mishap and firmly established the viability of the route for future trains. From 1859 through the first part of 1861, Hancock sent freight wagons over the Mojave Road on a regular basis [14].

Although the Mohaves had been subjugated and the Colorado crossing was now considered safe, Indian troubles in the Mojave Desert were not over. By 1860, the desert-dwelling "Pah-Utes" (Southern Paiutes, Chemehuevis and others) had become adept at waiting in ambush for stragglers and strays, striking swiftly and escaping to remote canyons with their victims. Horses and mules were taken, and ultimately, human lives as well, forcing the military once again to respond.

In the spring of 1860, the Los Angeles papers were filled with alarm at continuing Indian depredations to travelers. Particularly outrageous were the murders of three white men on the Salt Lake Trail (see map, pg. 28) purportedly by Paiute Indians. Responding to intense local pressure, General Clarke ordered Bvt. Major James H. Carleton to take Companies "B" and "K" of the 1st Dragoons from Fort Tejon into the Mojave "to punish the murderers and prevent the recurrence of such acts" (Mackall in 12). To that end, Carleton and his troops scoured the desert in search of Indians to punish and found a hapless few. On April 30, Carleton sent a detachment of sixteen dragoons with 1st Lieutenant Milton Carr to scout the Providence Mountains and Soda Springs. Carr's report (with emphasis added) includes a description of the construction of the first structure at Soda Springs.

Major;

I have the honor to state, that, in compliance with verbal orders from you, I left this camp at 4 O'Clock P.M. April 30th/60, with one Sergeant and fifteen men for Soda Springs to scout for Pah Ute Indians in the vicinity of the Sand-hills and Providence Mountains, also *to throw up a small redoubt at Soda Springs for the protection of travellers* . . .

May 1st. Left Camp at daylight and marched to Soda Springs, where I arrived at 11 O'Clock A.M. The wagon did not get in until 4 O'Clock P.M. the road being very sandy and rocky all the way. Found plenty of tule grass and water here. There are three springs, one large and two small ones. The water is impregnated with some alkaline substance and is unpleasant to the taste. Between the mouth of the Cañon and the springs, we crossed two old Indian trails, going in the direction of the Providence Mountains. Had the place for a small, circular redoubt marked out, to be thrown up by four men that were to remain with the wagon . . .

May 3rd. Left camp at 3 O'Clock A.M. and returned to Soda Springs to get water and rest the animals . . . On my arrival in camp at Soda Springs, I found the redoubt going up finely. The earth is very good for such purposes, being very tenacious and there is plenty of good sod for revetting. With plenty of tools and the necessary time, a very good and substantial redoubt could be built here.

May 6th. . . . Camp at Soda Spring . . . Found the redoubt about two-thirds finished. Put all of the men at work at it again . . .

May 8th. . . . Found the redoubt finished except the traverse in front of the entrance [Carr in 12].

On his second ten-day scouting expedition in the same area, Lt. Carr had his men finish the redoubt.

June 4th. Lay over to-day to rest the horses and finish the Redoubt. Had it finished so that a small party of men can hold it securely against any number of Indians that will ever be likely to be in that part of the country. Loop-holes are so arranged around the top, that men inside of the redoubt can command all the ground around, without exposing themselves to the fire of the Indians. Had the front traverse so arranged, also, that it will afford secure shelter to three or four horses [Carr in 12].

In a report to his superior, Carleton described Lt. Carr's accomplishments and the redoubt, which he named for Capt. Hancock in Los Angeles.

Figure 5. Redoubt at Camp Cady. Circa 1863. Photograph by Rudolph d'Heureuse. Courtesy of the Bancroft Library, University of California, Berkeley; Collection of T.P. Farquahar, 1963.

> The redoubt erected at Soda Spring is the same size as that erected at Bitter Spring: it is called *Hancock's Redoubt.* Should small parties hereafter be required to operate from that point, five or six men on foot in this redoubt can guard the supplies during the absence of the scouts. In this desert these redoubts will last for many years [Carleton in 12].

Unfortunately, this redoubt did not last long enough to have its appearance preserved for posterity. There are no known photographs or drawings of it, and no trace of this structure has been found at Soda Springs to date. Perhaps it looked something like the one built at Camp Cady and photographed by R. d'Heureuse in 1863. The main outpost at Camp Cady was located on the Mojave River a few miles east of modern Barstow.

A few months after the completion of Hancock's Redoubt, Carleton and his men withdrew to Fort Tejon, confident the problems with the Pah-Utes were over. In fact, the situation in the desert remained more or less unchanged, with Indian ambush a constant threat to those who traveled the Mojave Road. The beginning of the Civil War forced the abandonment of Carleton's outposts, and also Fort Mojave, for several years. The desert dwellers might have enjoyed another respite from the white man's incursions if a new irresistable force had not drawn men from all over California to the eastern edge of the desert—GOLD.

New Traffic: Prospectors

Once again, California was alive with the news—gold had been discovered, first in 1860 in Bear and Holcomb Valleys in the San Bernardino Mountains [49], then in 1861 at Eldorado Canyon along the Colorado River. When new placer deposits were found the following year in the mountains east of La Paz, also on the Colorado, the rush was on in earnest. Miners fanned out from the Colorado and made several new gold strikes in the mountains to the east. On February 24, 1863, President Lincoln signed into law the Act giving territorial status to Arizona [14]. Prescott was selected as the territorial capital and the nearby mines became the new destination for those on the Mojave Road.

Hundreds of miners in California eager to reach the new gold fields sought the easiest route across the desert to the river. Beginning in 1862, some used a new southern road to La Paz over San Gorgonio Pass by way of Dos Palmas and the Chuckwalla Bench. For a time this route was known as the "Bradshaw Road" as it was laid out by William D. Bradshaw and others [38]. It was also known as the La Paz Road (see Figure 4). Many other travelers stayed with the Mojave Road and found themselves at Soda Springs.

San Francisco *Bulletin*, July 31, 1863. Extract from a letter dated at Los Angeles, July 25, 1863.

The Fortune Seekers

At Soda Springs there was quite a show of immigration. The wagons, men, horses and camp fires looked very much like Sacramento in '49. They are all making their way to the Colorado mines, where they expect to make their fortunes; and will make them, too, if they are only prudent, sober, industrious and honest [15].

Traffic along the Mojave Road intensified with the increased demand for supplies and the flow of prospectors and miners. In 1863, Fort Mojave was regarrisoned and Fort Whipple was established near Prescott in Arizona to maintain the military as a buffer between zealous miners and dispossessed natives.

Dennis Casebier, Mojave Desert historian, has uncovered two narratives written by soldiers of the 4th Infantry, California Volunteers, on their way to regarrison Fort Mojave in 1863. Both contain interesting observations about the water at Soda

Springs, its properties and its temperature out of the ground. The first was written by Edward Carlson in May, 1863:

> Twenty miles more brought us to Soda Springs. This place is the last station before setting out for the longest stretch without water on this route. Out of a little hill of almost pure white quartz pours a large, warm spring. The water is as clear as crystal, but very disagreeable to the taste, as if mixed with sal soda and other salts. It must possess excellent medical properties, for as we had to make our next march by night, we rested for a day, and during this day I kept bathing my much swollen wounded leg, and with wonderful effect. It removed almost all the swelling and pain, and from that time on I had no difficulty in traveling [Carlson 1863 in 10].

The second description was written by another California Volunteer, Alonzo E. Davis.

> After we left the Mojave River, where we had an abundance of more or less alkalized water, we came to Soda Lake, after a very hot march . . . The water was warm and contained soda and other minerals to such a degree that it was not at all palatable. Take a glass of milk-warm water, add a pinch of salt and a teaspoon of soda, and you will have a very fair sample of Soda Lake water.
>
> This lake was so-called from the fact that about six miles from shore to shore, where the wagon road crosses, it is covered with an incrustation that puffs up so that you sink into it as you would in soft snow. It was as white, too, from the soda that had risen. This soda answers quite well for raising biscuits, especially if you have a sourdough starter, as I have eaten the bread [Davis 1863 in 10].

In July of the following year, Professor B. Silliman "visited the Colorado river for the purpose of seeing some of the mineral districts near Fort Mojave." Prof. Silliman, a geologist, was among the first to look at Soda Springs from a scientist's perspective.

> The distance from Los Angeles to the Colorado is about 250 miles, which we made in nine encampments. Few of the stations on this route are laid down on any of the published maps, and are generally watering places only, the whole distance being an uninhabited wilderness, nearly destitute of the means of supporting life . . .
>
> Soda Springs marks the site of an ancient lake, the surface of the saline plane being as level as the sea. A powerful spring of calcareous water breaks out on its western margin, charged with sulphate of lime, and bearing, among the

ignorant guides of these desert regions, the reputation of containing arsenic or some deadly metallic poison. We drank freely of it, however, with no ill effects to man or beast, and were very glad to obtain so potable a water after several days of great dearth of this essential of comfort.

The term 'Soda Spring' is a misnomer, as the water is destitute both of carbonic acid and alkalinity (it did not affect reddened litmus); has doubtless received its name from its bright sparkling appearance, so much in contrast with the green stagnant water of the 'government holes,' or wells, dug by the roadside for the supply of travellers.

A gigantic fly abounds at Soda Springs and Marl Springs. They were such an annoyance to our animals as to compel us in each case to move on before we were ready, to avoid the torments they inflicted on the poor beasts with their sharp lancets, drawing blood every time when, with a droning sound like that of a bumble bee, they struck the skin. They seem to attack the animals in preference to men, as none of our party suffered from them [57].

From these descriptions, it would appear that a traveler's opinion of the taste of the water at Soda Springs rose in proportion to the level of his thirst. It is also worth noting that beginning in the 1860s, the main stream of water at Soda Springs was reported as flowing out of the rock with some force; this is not the case in modern times. There is a round opening in the limestone at ground level behind the present dining room of the Desert Studies Center which is said to be the hole from which the water flowed. Today there is usually a small amount of water in the bottom of this hole.

In an anonymous letter to the San Francisco *Alta California* dated June 14, 1866, another traveler complained of the taste and temperature of Soda Springs water in the quaint journalistic prose of the times.

Soda and Salt. From Camp Cady to Soda Lake, a distance of forty miles, the road is, for the most part, heavy with sand. "Soda Lake" is, as its name indicates, a lake of soda; here it is about six miles in width. Looking out over its glistening whiteness, were it not for the blistering rays of old "Sol," that seem to come down here with intensified fierceness, one might imagine himself in the land of sleigh bells.

A spring of water boils out from beneath a marble mountain, sparkling and bright, and looks so inviting to a thirsty stranger, that he is on his knees, and has gulped down a gill of warm water, seasoned with a little salt and more soda, be-

Figure 6. "Warm Soda Springs". Circa 1863. Photograph by Rudolph d'Heureuse. Courtesy of the Bancroft Library, University of California, Berkeley; Collection of T.P. Farquahar, 1963.

fore he has detected the cheat. I should like much to see the piety of some good Dominie put to the test here. If he did not ejaculate something about that hot place that is supposed to have something to do with warming this water, I should be ready to declare that Pluto's claim was small on him indeed [15].

Through the 1860s, as military and civilian traffic across the Mojave increased to an all-time high, the threat of ambush by desert Indians likewise escalated. Mail service was disrupted and stock losses mounted. Reports of attacks on wagon trains filled the papers, arousing public sentiment. The problems with the Pah-Utes once again called for a military solution. Camp Cady, east of Barstow on the Mojave River, was regarrisoned in June, 1866 [14] though the troops could do little more than provide mounted escorts for the mail carriers.

Hancock's Redoubt was not regarrisoned at the same time as Camp Cady in 1866, perhaps because there was no longer a redoubt left there to reoccupy. On April 21, 1867, General James F. Rusling visited Soda Springs while conducting an inspection tour of posts across the west for the Quartermaster-General's Office in Washington D.C. According to Rusling's description of the site (quoted below, emphasis added), there were no structures at Soda Springs at this time.

There is the possibility that Rusling and company unknowingly camped at the spring on the **south** end of Limestone Hill, as they had approached the site from the south. He may not have seen the remains of the redoubt in the notch on the north end, its hypothesized location. In his account Rusling sounds somewhat disoriented.

> Skirting the borders of it [Soda Lake], we reached a rocky bluff on (I think) the northern shore, and there found a noble spring of excellent water, welling up from unknown depths, within a stone's throw of the soda deposits. Here was the usual halting place, and as we had driven all night, we went into camp on arriving there, soon after sunrise. It was Sunday, April 21; *there was no house or even hut there;* no person or living thing; and what with the heat, and glare, and awful desolation—our weariness, fatigue, and sense of isolation—I think it was about the most wretched and miserable day I ever spent anywhere [53].

Not long after Rusling's tour of inspection, the decision was made to reestablish the outpost at Soda Springs to provide a change of horses for escort riders [69]. The first attempt to carry out this decision was apparently not successful, as troops were there only for a few weeks in the spring of 1867. The army persevered, however, and a few months later, Lt. Manuel Eyre reestablished the post at Soda Springs using men from Camp Cady. It remained manned almost continuously until May 23, 1868, when it was abandoned by the army permanently [13].

In a letter dated August 24, 1867, Major William R. Price recommended that a blockhouse and corral be constructed at Soda Springs similar to ones he was having built at Beale's Spring and Willow Grove in Arizona [13]. By November of 1867, "a small stone shanty furnished quarters for the detachment of six men from Camp Cady" (report of Major Henry M. Robert in 11). This stone house is the first of its kind known to have been built at Soda Springs. An army inspection made March 27, 1868 reported "one corporal and three privates from Camp Cady were occupying one house made of stone and earth" at Soda Springs. A corral had also been constructed at the site [10].

It is believed by many that a portion of the lower walls of this first stone building are still standing at Soda Springs, east of the main diningroom and north of the kitchen. These may be the ruins Helen Springer described in 1969. A professional study of this structure is needed to resolve the question.

Despite the improved accommodations, in 1867 the comfort level at the outpost must have been quite low, as the garrison was plagued by desertions; "In fact, Soda Lake's entire detachment deserted en masse on one occasion" [69]. Although later writers have fancied the name "Fort Soda" for the outpost [32, 65], the site never held that name in any official document.

On October 16, 1867, a tragedy occurred which put Soda Springs back in the headlines. A party of three men traveling with the mail buggy was attacked by Indians on foot in Afton Canyon, some 14 miles west of Soda Springs. The buggy driver Sam Button whipped up his team and made a run for the safety of Soda Springs which they reached without further incident. However, one of the passengers, Army surgeon Dr. Merrill E. Shaw, had been mortally wounded in the neck by an Indian arrow in the inital attack. He died the next day and was buried at Soda Springs [14]. Many months later, when Shaw's relatives requested his remains for reburial back East, their exact resting spot could not be relocated. There is some reason to believe that Dr. Shaw's remains still lie below the ground somewhere at Soda Springs (Casebier, personal communication, 1981).

In 1868, the trans-desert mail and military freight route was shifted south to the La Paz Road (or Bradshaw Trail) and the need for army escorts across the Mojave ended. Camp Cady remained an army post until April 24, 1871, when the troops were withdrawn [14]. Lt. James Halloran supervised the sale of the government property at Camp Cady to stockmen Mr. T. John Cantell and Mr. Winters [52]. From 1871 on, civilian traffic to the mines and points east replaced military convoys on the Mojave Road.

Civilians Take Over: The Stages and Stationkeepers

With the end of the Civil War and the pacification of the desert Indians, the 1870s opened an era of rapid growth for southern California with a copy of Charles Nordhoff's 1873 best-seller "California for Travellers and Settlers" firmly in hand, many a winter-weary Easterner came west to enjoy the "exquisite and unalloyed pleasures" of California for himself [48]. Early in the 1870s the first Washington Navel oranges were planted in Riverside and when the fruit ripened in the winter of 1878, a new boom industry was created which attracted settlers in large numbers [50]. Ranchers and homesteaders arrived in the desert as well, filing claims on land along the Mojave River, giving birth to desert communities which eventually grew into the towns of Victorville, Hesperia, Daggett and Barstow.

After the withdrawal of troops from the desert in 1871, Soda Springs (generally known as "Soda Lake Station" during these years) was occupied sporadically by civilian stationkeepers. A description of the waystation was published in the San Bernardino *Guardian* on August 30, 1871 in a letter entitled "Jottings by the Way En Route to Ivanpah, Clark District." This letter (with original spelling, etc. preserved) also includes the first known reference to a public bath at Soda Springs.

> [Coming from Afton Canyon] we . . . then passed on to the Soda Lake station, where we arrived about 11 o'clock and were agreeable surprised by Messrs. Ward & Co., to find that they had things arranged so well in such a God-forsaken country. The house is built at the end of a small rocky hill detached from the main line of hills, the road running on both sides of the hill.
>
> Close to the house a large spring bursts forth from among the rocks sending quite a respectable stream. The boys have built for the use of the public a nice bathing place and invited us to take a bath while they were preparing dinner. We lost no time in availing ourselves of the opportunity and if you should ever travel this road you will think the same as we did arriving there covered with dust and perspiring freely that it is really a luxury, however the water is impregnated with alkali, soda, etc., and has a peculiar sweetish taste and does not seem to satisfy thirst; the animals drank very little [San Bernardino *Guardian* Aug. 30, 1871, G. Moon Collection].

From the standpoint of traffic on the Mojave Road, the biggest development of the 1870s was the opening of rich silver mining districts in the New York, Providence and Clark Mountain areas. The Piute Mining Company first staked claims and laid out the town of Ivanpah on the east side of Clark Mountain in 1869, and soon men were flocking to the mines. By August of 1871, the town of Ivanpah had a hotel and two stores and by September, 1875, a population of 60 to 80 men. Many freight wagon loads of ore and supplies were shipped in and out of Ivanpah during the next twenty years. Mining at Ivanpah continued into the 1890s [67].

No longer fearing attack from hostile Indians and spurred on by visions of unlimited wealth, prospectors spread out across the desert, probing even the most remote spots. Emigrants and traders took to the road as well, a number of whom must have stopped at Soda Springs, though first-hand accounts are scarce. A group of travelers at the station can be seen in a photograph dated 1874 (Figure 7). In 1875, regular stagecoach service between Prescott and San Bernardino was established, with stops at the major water holes [14].

Figure 7. Soda Springs Station in 1874. Reagles Collection; Courtesy of the Fort Verde State Park, Camp Verde, Arizona.

For the tax year 1874–1875, a Mr. Smith Haile of San Bernardino was the stationkeeper at Soda Springs, as indicated by the San Bernardino County Assessor's records (Feldhym Library Collection).

Haile, Smith

Residence, Soda Lake
Soda Lake Station, real estate value $50
2 wagons $200
5 harness $40
1 Spanish horse $20
8 mules $600
Total personal property $860
Total property value $910
Road and poll tax paid $1 each
Total tax $22.75

A long-shot advertisement placed in a Barstow newspaper in 1982 by this author turned up a previously unknown diary of a trip over the Mojave Road in January of 1880. The account, written by 20-year old Ralph Benson, was accompanied by a pen-and-ink sketch entitled "Soda Lake Station," the first drawing to be located in the documentary record.

The "station" was drawn by Benson as a single rectangular structure divided down the center by a breeze-way. Based on shape and window depth, this building may yet stand at Soda Springs. It may be the core of the structure which currently houses the store and Desert Studies office. From his diary entry, Ralph Benson was clearly not much impressed by Soda Springs.

> *Jan. 22.* After a long hard pull through deep sand, we arrived at the edge of Soda Lake . . . Driving along the edge a mile or two, we came to Soda Lake Station, where there is a strong spring running out at the foot of a little hill. The water is very clear and pure to the eye, but to the taste it has no chill, and is strongly impregnated with Alkali—so strong that when we squeezed the juice from a Lime into a cup of it, we could still taste the alkali badly. The limes were not equal to the emergency.
>
> Lizzie draws her face up in wrinkles and contemptuously declares that it is "miserable stuff" while Frank and I smile at her woebegone visage as we sip the alkalescent liquid, observing that it is not as bad as we had anticipated.
>
> The station keeper is a hard looking case; but perhaps that is due to his surroundings, for they are severe and desolate to the extreme. Here death and desolation hold undisputed sway . . . [Benson Journal, Duffield-Stoll Collection].

A reference from the *Calico Print* newspaper dated August 3, 1882, identifies another former stationkeeper at Soda Springs as Mr. George Hetzel and suggests that as of this date the station may have been abandoned. Considering the month (August) and likely average daytime temperatures (110° +), this would not be surprising.

> The wife of Mr. Geo Hetzel and his daughter are camped near Medlin's while he is in S.B. attending to business mat-

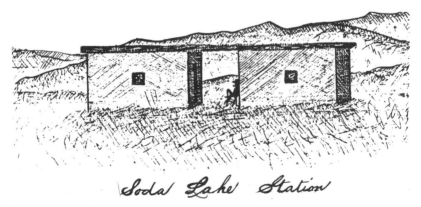

Soda Lake Station

Figure 8. Earliest known drawing of Station at Soda Springs. Ralph Benson, 1880. Courtesy of the Pollard Family.

ters. For the last eight months Mr. Hetzel kept the station at Soda Lake, but as there was not travel enough through there to make it pay, he left a few days ago and is on his way with his family to the coast [*Calico Print*, G. Moon Collection, Mojave River Valley Museum, Barstow].

Three years later, on March 1, 1885, Soda Springs was again occupied, this time by parties interested in local mining prospects. A letter written by a visitor and describing the site, then known as "Shenandoah Camp," was first published in the *Calico Print* newspaper. The author, "Moss Agate," so far from objecting to the taste of Soda Springs water, calls it the "water of life," another first for the historic record.

Soda Lake Mines—Shenandoah Camp, Soda Lake District-Feb. 23, 1885.

Editor Print—I have been prospecting in Soda Lake district for about a month and as I have not seen any accounts of the same in your valuable paper I thought I would send you the following items:

I would like to enlighten the numerous mining camps of the great Mojave desert in regard to the prospects of Soda Lake district, which possesses indications of immense hidden wealth unsurpassed in the history of mining. The old Government road passes through the district, which lies about 60 miles east of Daggett. Miles and miles of mineralized rock can be seen on the earth surface, a most interesting [sight] to the gold and silver seeker's eye. At present there are only a few prospectors in the district . . .

On leaving the Iron King we continued our way southward a short distance and came in sight of Colonel Smith's camp. In the distance can be seen the extensive Soda Lake placer claims laid off, with stakes standing up like the stones in a graveyard.

After passing around a point of the mountains we came to a habitation of ancient design, which might easily be imagined to be the one the famous Jack built. Knocking, the informal welcome, "come in," was heard within. Our friends, the Harts, were at home. Although friends on short acquaintance, we were made to feel entirely at home by them, Col. Smith and Mr. Anderson, with the hospitality for which Southern gentlemen are noted, and the repast spread before us would tempt the gods.

After our appetites, made keen by a long day's travel, were appeased, the evening was sociably spent in conversation, occasionally regaling ourselves with old Kentucky peach brandy and smoking fragrant cigars, besides in-

dulging in quaffs from the "water of life." You would not object to the celestial name given the liquid should you see
the living spring of mineral water just outside the cabin
door, that discharges about twenty miners' inches of hot
water per minute. It is health producing and life-preserving
to any person that partakes of it. A pool has been dug out
large enough for five or six persons to bathe in, the water
flowing in and out of the pool continually.

About 10 o'clock we consigned ourselves to the embraces
of Morpheus with his phantastic dreams, and were awak-
ened at early morn by the mellifluous quacking of the wild
ducks and mudhens and the prolonged strains of the gay
and festive burro. After breakfast we took a look at the
Shenandoah mine, accompanied by Mr. Anderson, which is
just south of the house and springs . . .

I will close by stating that a town site has been staked off,
for it is expected that a thriving mining camp will be established here in the near future . . . [*Calico Print*, G. Moon
Collection, Mojave River Valley Museum, Barstow].

"Moss Agate" was certainly a master of hyperbole; no
"town" ever materialized at Soda Springs, and Colonel Alonzo
Smith and associates must have moved on to greener pastures
shortly thereafter, as they left no paper trail in the area after the
year 1885.

CHAPTER FIVE

Miners, Railroads and Homesteads
1886 to 1936

Although the claims for the area did not pan out as initially promised, prospectors continued to work in this part of the desert through the 1890s. Soda Springs was included within the Solo Mining District as defined by M. H. Powell, S. N. Morris, Frank Murphy, Thomas Stafford and Frank Riggs at their first meeting on January 12, 1886 (Misc. D:445 SB County Records). The last miner listed, Frank **Riggs,** is an important name for Soda Springs during this period.

Frank Riggs and his wife, Sarah, filed their first mining claim in San Bernardino County on December 12, 1882 (Mines C:344 SB County Records) and spent the next 35 years locating and working mines, mainly near their camp east of Silver Lake. In October, 1887, the Riggs were apparently living in a house at Soda Springs, as a claim filed on that date for Mojave River water mentions them.

> Notice: I claim the water flowing in the channel, or bed of the Mojave River opposite this notice, to the extent of 600 inches, miners measure. Said water to be conveyed into a 12-inch pipe under a pressure of 32 inches and to be conveyed to a point on Soda Lake 1 mile south or southwest from **Riggs House,** and to be used for milling and irrigating purposes, and such other domestic use as may be necessary . . . This claim is situated about two or two and a half miles below Old Caves Station on the Mojave River, San Bernardino County. P. H. Newhill [SB County Water Record C:240].

Two years later, on November 5, 1889, Frank and Sarah Riggs filed a claim on the "Hetzel Mill Site," being "five acres with springs and pools of water, earth and rocks thereon . . . and may be particularly described as embracing within its surface limits the buildings and other

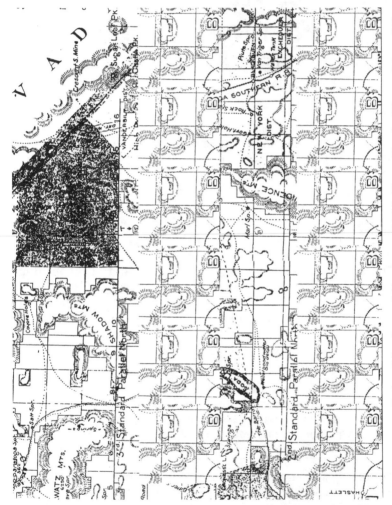

Figure 9. Solo Mining District and Environs, 1896. From Perris Miners Map of the Desert Region of Southern California, 1896.

improvements known as Soda Lake Station" (SB County Water Record C:570). Possibly the Hetzel Mill Site was located at the springs on the south end of Limestone Hill, as there are rock and concrete foundations to be seen there today which may well have been built to support a milling operation. It is also possible that these remains date to a later period, during the tenure of the Pacific Salt and Soda Company (see below). A careful investigation by an historical archaeologist could answer the question.

Returning to the Riggs, they are rather mysterious desert figures, and naturally, ignorance has led to speculation. There are few facts known of their personal history beyond those recorded by the census enumerators in 1900 and 1910. Frank, a "mining expert," was born in Michigan in November, 1845. Sarah was also born in Michigan in February, 1844 and was the mother of four children, none of whom apparently lived with them in the desert. The two are thought to have made a fortune from their various silver mines [67] but if so, they don't appear to have spent it in the desert. Sarah Riggs died in 1914 and the last mining claim entry for Frank is dated October 11, 1917 [33].

In 1898 Frank and Sarah Riggs filed a water claim on property one-half mile north of Soda Springs which they called "upper Badger Holes." The spot today is along Zzyzx Road in an area of perennial seepage crossed by a metal culvert.

> Notice is hereby given that we the undersigned in conformity with law hereby locate and claim (100) miners inches of water to be developed at these springs for the purpose of watering Horses, cattle and other live stock and for irrigation and other domestic uses and purposes. We also claim Ten acres of land upon which these springs are situated to be used for the proper development and distribution of said water.

> These springs are situated about one half mile Northerly from Soda Lake Station in San Bernardino County, California, and are known as the upper "Badger Holes." Located this 14th day of June, 1898 by Frank and Sarah Riggs [SB Water Record F:230].

The Riggs' interest in the water at Soda Springs is not readily explained by their presumed domestic needs. Not long after filing the claim to the water at the upper Badger Holes, Frank and Sarah Riggs recorded the location of a camp near their Silver Lake mines which they called "Silurian Camp" (SB Records Mines 252:224). Their presence there in the 1900 and 1910 census indicates that their main residence was at Silurian Camp, near their rich Alta Group mines, not at Soda Springs.

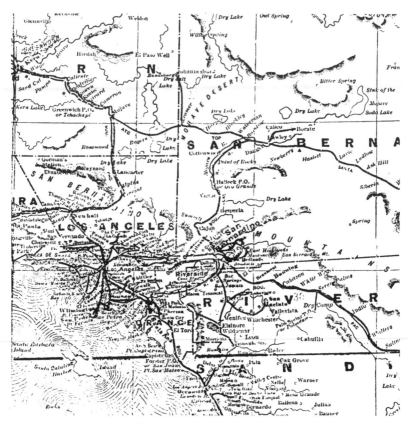

Figure 10. Principle railroad routes in Southern California, 1899.

The remains of an arrastra were found near Zzyzx Road during the 1960s (now gone, though the stones and a photograph remain). The Riggs' nearby water and mill site claims suggest they were interested in Soda Springs because they were refining their silver ore there. Perhaps they built the arrastra on Zzyzx Road? The abundant water made it a desirable location for simple ore refining using the arrastra method.

> An arrastra is one of the simplest methods of pulverizing and amalgamating auriferous quartz [or other ore-bearing rock]. It was invented, or re-invented, centuries ago by the Mexicans, and consists of a circular bed from eight to twenty feet across, paved with stones, in which quartz that has been broken into small pieces by a sledge hammer is placed and slowly ground to dust by the dragging of a large "muller" or slab of granite over the quartz-covered pavement . . . If the quartz is not very hard it can be pulverized in four or five hours.

> The ore is kept wet all the time, and the grinding is continued until the mass is like cream. Quicksilver is then put in . . . and the grinding goes on for an hour or two longer until the amalgamation is considered complete. Quite a stream of water is then allowed to run in through a sluice gate, and the grinding continues half an hour, to let the amalgam settle in the bottom. Grinding then stops. Another gate is opened, and the stream of water soon washes out the fine gray mud to which the rock has been reduced, leaving the metal on the bed of the arrastra [56].

Although many clearly recognized its resources, it appears that by 1900 Soda Springs was again empty of permanent residents. The era of the stagecoach had faded with the coming of the railroad in 1883. Traffic on the Mojave Road dwindled to a trickle as faster, easier routes of travel were pioneered. Interest in the Solo (or Soda Lake) Mining District continued through the turn of the century, but languished compared to other areas for lack of cheap transportation. An article in the Needles *Eye* dated May 14, 1904, expressed the common complaint of miners in the Mojave.

> It has been known for years that many exceedingly rich specimens of ore have been found in this isolation, yet these prospects have been unable of development because of the scarcity of wood, water and the great and expensive distance through which mining supplies would have to be taken . . . The Soda Lake district stands particularly noticeable in this respect . . . [G. Moon Collection, Mojave River Valley Museum, Barstow].

The Tonopah & Tidewater Railroad Arrives

The solution to the transportation problem in the East Mojave was the brainchild of one of this state's great entrepreneurs in the old-school capitalist tradition, Francis Marion Smith, nicknamed "Borax" Smith. In 1906 construction began on Smith's Tonopah and Tidewater Railroad, built initially to replace the rustic but exceptionally inefficient twenty-mule teams in the job of hauling borax to market from Smith's mines near Death Valley [33]. From its completion in 1907, the Tonopah and Tidewater (or "T & T" as it was known to most) functioned as a regional lifeline, spanning some 250 miles of desert between Ludlow and Goldfield, Nevada. Track was laid through Soda Springs and out on the berm across Soda Lake through the spring of 1906.

Figure 11. Reprint of a T & T railroad advertisement, 1908. Courtesy of the Hugh Tolford Collection.

The Tonopah and Tidewater Railroad averaged one train daily through Soda Springs from 1907 to 1940, though its most active, prosperous years were between 1908 and 1914 [45]. Its last day of operation was June 14, 1940 and by July, 1943, the tracks and rails were removed for the war effort. Its main success financially was in hauling freight, and for a time the

Figure 12. Soda Works at Soda Lake taken from T & T railroad line. Circa 1908. Taken by Frank Green. Courtesy of the Hugh Tolford Collection.

prospects looked good for a profitable soda works at Soda Lake which would use the T & T to ship its products. No doubt these prospects influenced the choice of routing. A flurry of activity at Soda Springs seems to have followed the construction of the Tonopah & Tidewater in 1907, resulting in a number of improvements to the site.

> San Bernardino *Sun*, August 11, 1907—Booster Edition. [A trip over the Tonopah & Tidewater]
>
> *Over Soda Beds* - The next development is that being made by the Pacific Salt and Soda Co. at Soda Lake. The railroad passes through this wonderful deposit of almost pure soda for a distance of nearly 12 miles, and the road bed is made of this great component of the American biscuit. The company is building large evaporating beds into which the waters of the lake will be pumped and then allowed to evaporate under the influence of the solar rays. Large furnaces are being constructed in which the deposit will be refined for table use.
>
> Splendid stone buildings are being constructed on the site of the old fort that was established here by the great pathfinder, Fremont [sic], and in close proximity to the great Soda Springs. The company doing this work must not be confounded with the Pacific Coast Soda Co. The Pacific Salt and Soda Co. has no stock for sale. It is a closed corporation that is working the deposit [Haenszel Collection].

This quote is noteworthy for the mention of construction taking place at that time (1907). In 1953, author L. Burr Belden asserted that the buildings at Soda Springs dated from previous occupation of the site.

> Five miles south of Baker, on the west side of the glaring white surface of Soda Lake was a station named Soda. It was an old stone fortification left over from Indian war days and had been a stop for stages on the Old Government road. The fort had been built by Col. Carlton and named Hancock Redoubt.
>
> Now, when the T & T was built it housed an old man who lived there as a hermit. He was said to have shot at strangers through the loopholes of the ancient redoubt . . . Many a T & T freight crew stopped their train while all hands took a swim at Soda during hot summer days [3].

Burr Belden again mentioned Soda Springs in another article dated three years later. He noticed that Soda Springs was shown on a 1902 map labeled as "Govt. Sta. Water." Belden felt that the name "tends to confirm reports from persons who constructed the Tonopah & Tidewater past the site that a considerable portion of **two** stone buildings remained at the Fort Soda site" from previous occupations [4].

It is possible that Belden was correct and that the structure (or structures) seen at Soda Springs in 1907 were remnants of those constructed by Lt. Manuel Eyre and his men in 1867 which were being remodeled for new uses. Other writers believed, however, that "most remains of old buildings at Soda Springs only date back to the building of the T & T" [35].

To be sure, Smith's railroad itself was not involved in any building construction, as it had neither motive nor budget to improve the facilities at Soda Springs. Beyond laying track, the T & T did little more than reuse what it found there. The raised berm of the Tonopah and Tidewater Railroad track is still visible at Soda Springs today; part of it to the north of the main entrance road was widened in modern times to serve as a landing strip for light planes.

The sole improvment constructed by the Tonopah & Tidewater Railroad at Soda Springs was a short eight-car spur with a switch for changing tracks. Also, for a few short months, there was a station of sorts at Soda Lake which must have made use of a structure already present at the site. It was opened on November 30, 1907 and closed for good on August 31, 1908. The sole station agent listed was R. H. Blee (Transit Book, Hugh Tolford Collection). Perhaps Mr. Blee was the same man referred to by Burr Belden as the "hermit."

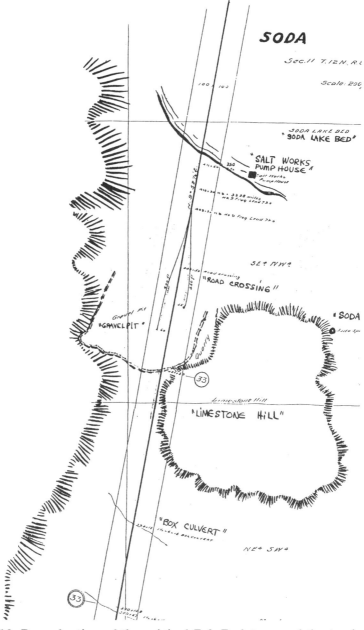

Figure 13. Reproduction of the original T & T plat map of the track through Soda Lake Station. Circa 1908. Courtesy of Hugh Tolford Collection.

Salt and Soda from Soda Lake

As described in the *Sun* article from 1907, the Pacific Salt and Soda Company was the name of the concern working the deposits in Soda Lake at that time. They reported recovering a small quantity of salt the following year, although the operation was not in full production [66]. It appears the company did invest considerable funds and effort to get the operation going.

> **Soda Lake Camp:** to extract sodium carbonate, which was used in a variety of products, from baking powder to paint, the Pacific Coast Soda Company in 1908 built a plant and a 2-mile narrow-gauge railroad running to huge outdoor vats near the old adobe station. Since soda works were highly mechanized, the camp probably remained very small. The operation apparently shut down after only a year.
>
> The old vats remain near the abandoned grade of the Tonopah & Tidewater Railroad [34].

The "vats" referred to are more commonly described as evaporating ponds, large rectangular areas with low earthen walls and removeable wooden sluice gates, several of which are still visible at Soda Springs to the north, east and southeast of Limestone Hill (see pg. 59.) The berm and several ties and spikes from the narrow-gauge railroad can also still be found on the northern border of the site. The Pacific Salt and Soda Company apparently remained interested in the deposits at Soda Lake through 1911 although only working there sporadically during that time.

> **August 25, 1911:** SALT & SODA. On the T & T R.R. north of Crucero are located the works of the Pacific Salt and Soda Co . . . The grounds cover 7,000 acres and the capacity of the plant is 10,000 tons per month. About $50,000 have been expended on the plant. It yields main values in high grade salt, being a great deposit in the bed of a dry lake.
>
> The Company has just purchased a 32 h.p. gasoline engine to pump brine. Officers and directors reside in Los Angeles. They hope to be in full operation this fall [Barstow *Printer*, G. Moon Collection, Mojave River Valley Museum, Barstow].

In 1912, the news was again hopeful; "New blood has been interested in the company and more activity is expected soon" (Barstow *Printer*, Jan. 5, 1912). If indeed the company became more active, it was not at Soda Springs.

During the tenure of the Pacific Salt and Soda Company at Soda Springs, a report of a visit to the site was written by Walter C. Mendenhall for the U.S. Geological Survey and published in 1909. No mention is made of the soda works; the springs may have been deserted. This account is the first to provide the dimensions of the bathing pool and confirms the presence of more than one stone building at the site.

Government Well at Soda Lake, San Bernardino County. At Soda Lake, a station on the Tonopah and Tidewater Railroad, is one of the wells dug by government troops forty or fifty years ago. It is on the eastern branch of the old emigrant road from San Bernardino to Salt Lake City by way of the Mohave River, and is near the west edge of the sink of the Mohave, at the eastern base of the Soda Lake Mountains.

The well is easily found, because its position is marked by the ruins of the old adobe and stone buildings erected by the troops. The water is a part of the underflow of the Mohave River, and is of fair quality, in spite of the heavy deposits of soda that whiten the surface all about it.

The well is a pool lined with stone, about 5 by 8 feet in dimensions and 3 feet deep. It is near the edge of some tules about 150 feet southeast of the largest stone building. The buildings are on the north side of a limestone knob, and the traveler can not see them from the road until he is within 100 yards of them. This knob, however, near the middle of the western edge of Soda Lake, serves as a guide to their position. The tules, which can be seen from a distance as one approaches the well, also aid in finding it [40].

The First Religious Colony at Soda Springs

After about 1912, when the Pacific Salt and Soda Company's grand plans for the development of the soda apparently evaporated, references to Soda Springs in the historic record become quite scarce. The Mojave Road was no longer carrying trans-desert traffic and the area was only sparsely settled; the boom times in the desert were over. By 1914, the main borax mines near Death Valley were exhausted, as were the gold districts of Bullfrog and Rhyolite, and the T & T Railroad was obliged to abandon some of its trackage and regroup [45]. For the time being, the nation's attention had turned away from the desert toward pressing foreign affairs and the impending war with Germany.

The next residents of Soda Springs may well have been responding to international events in moving there, but the whole story is not known.

> A German group came along in 1914 and tried extracting quicksilver from Soda Lake. They ran the hermit off, built the old fort's walls higher and roofed it. The quicksilver operation was a failure and the Germans turned to manufacture of soda and salt only to have their operation halted when the United States declared war on Germany. The soda project was never revived after the armistice [3].

Comparing this version of events with the next, there appears to be some mixture of the facts which has yet to be sorted out.

> About the time of the first World War, a religious colony occupied the area near Soda Springs. The founder, Pastor Charles T. Russell, claimed that he was guided to the place by a vision that he would find gold in the nearby hills to finance his colony. German aliens among the colonists involved the whole group in trouble. Russell was imprisoned along with several members of the colony and the offending Germans. The religious leader died October 30, 1916, and the Soda Springs settlement was abandoned.

> Russell and his converts built five frame houses at Soda Springs and spent $50,000 in an effort to mine gold in the adjacent mountains. The houses later were torn down and used in building the first structures at Baker, a few miles to the north [35].

Attempts to verify this story have turned up some otherwise unexplained evidence at Soda Springs and a small amount of information about the man, Charles Taze Russell. Pastor Charles T. Russell was born in Pittsburgh, Pennsylvania on February 16, 1852; his mother died when he was 9 years old. In 1884, Pastor Russell founded the Watchtower Bible and Tract Society, the legal agency of the Jehovah's Witnesses, of which he was president until his death on October 31, 1916 [1]. Several tenants of the Jehovah's Witnesses faith have brought the group notoriety through the years, among them the refusal to pledge an oath of allegiance, to vote, or to serve in the armed forces.

In his book, *The Object and Manner of the Lord's Return,* written in 1877, Pastor Russell predicted that Christ would make his invisible return to this world after a "40-Year Harvest of the Souls" which began in 1874. Thus, Russell calculated that the Lord's return would occur on October 1, 1914, about the time Russell and his followers are thought to have arrived at Soda Springs.

As to the evidence at Soda Springs, the remains of five rectangular poured concrete foundations have been found north of the entrance road and west of the main pond. They are badly cracked and deteriorated and appear to pre-date the modern construction period, which began in 1944. Also, near the Soda Springs Rockshelter, the word "BETHEL" can still be seen painted in white on a limestone rock face. This word means "House of God" in Hebrew and signifies a hallowed or holy place. Bethel was the name of a town in biblical Palestine some eleven miles north of Jerusalem which once briefly housed the Ark of the Covenant [1]; the name reputedly has a special significance for members of the Jehovah's Witnesses.

Whether Pastor Russell's death in 1916 or other pressures caused the group to leave, by the time of the next reported visit to the site in 1917, Soda Springs was again empty of residents.

Soda Springs Abandoned

The next visitor to the site was geologist David G. Thompson, who was conducting a "geographic, geologic, and hydrologic reconnaissance of the Mohave Desert Region" for the U.S. Geological Survey. In the course of his research, Thompson stopped at Soda Springs at least twice, in 1917 and again in 1919, both times recording important observations at the site.

> At Soda station there is a hill of limestone several hundred feet in diameter, which is separated from the main mountain mass by an alluvium-filled area about 100 yards wide. The alluvium probably represents a beach that was formed when a perennial lake covered the area.
>
> Two or more springs flow from the east side of the limestone hill. The water appears to seep directly from the rock about 5 feet above the surface of the playa. An abundance of tules and salt grass around the base of the hill shows that the seepage occurs over a larger area than indicated by the few openings that have been cleared out.
>
> The largest spring flows into a concrete reservoir about 15 by 30 feet in area and 5 feet deep. When visited in 1917 a small ram pumped water from this reservoir to an elevated tank for domestic use, but it had been removed when visited in 1919 [62].

A report by Thompson from a separate government publication provided much less detailed information on the water but a bit more area history.

> **Soda Station.** Water of poor quality at spring on east side of low limestone hill on east side of track. Several flowing wells are located on the south side of this hill. The water from these wells is practically as bad as that from the spring.
>
> At one time a religious colony formed a settlement at this place, but in December, 1919, the place was deserted [61].

The Quiet Decades

Through the 1920s, there are no reports from Soda Springs itself, although there were new neighbors just a few miles distant. Beginning just after the turn of the century, during what apparently was a wet cycle when desert agriculture looked more promising, hopeful farmers had moved to the Lanfair Valley east of Soda Springs, and also into the area near the Sink of the Mojave to settle and raise crops. The homesteaders southwest of Soda Springs clustered around the place where the Tonopah and Tidewater Railroad crossed what is now the Union Pacific track, a spot appropriately called "Crucero," meaning cross. Through the years 1911 to 1920, hundreds of people filed homestead claims to the land around Crucero, but only a few stayed to brave the sandy winds and summer heat.

One man who brought his family out in 1917 and did stay on was Elmo Proctor. He and his family toughed it out in Crucero until in 1921 his claim was "proved" and the land belonged to him. Then in 1925 when the Arrowhead Trail (later Highway 91) connecting Los Angeles with Salt Lake City was built through the Cronese basin, Elmo moved his family there and opened one of the first gas stations on the new highway between Daggett and Las Vegas [18]. Two previous alignments of the highway can still be seen from Interstate 15 as it crosses the Cronese basin, approximately six miles southwest of Zzyzx Road.

Although highway-building across the Mojave continued through the 1920s, activity in general was at a low level in the desert. Sections of railroad to played-out mining camps were torn up and empty towns abandoned. Most of the homesteading dry farmers gave up and moved out during the late 1920s, with the post office in Lanfair Valley closing on January 31, 1927 [27].

Figure 14. "Fort Soda Lake". Published in 1938 Barstow Printer Review, Travel Log #24 (Sept., 1940). Courtesy of the Mojave River Valley Museum Association #81 4337.

A few settlers returned to reoccupy empty cabins during the Depression, perhaps to try a little mining to get through the hard times. Cattle ranching operations continued in the East Mojave, though on a smaller scale from the days of the big outfits, like the Rock Springs Land and Cattle Co. [38].

A later visitor to Soda Springs paints a picture of what it was like there through the 1920s and 1930s.

> **Fort Rarely Visited.** After the construction of the Tonopah and Tidewater railway in 1907, different corporations made futile efforts to profitably gather and refine the salines in the lake bed. They expended much money in drilling wells, constructing on the lake bed large vats to evaporate brine and building mills.
>
> For some reason they never made profits and only the ruin of their fruitless efforts remain. Even the railway has been abandoned and some day its road bed will form an auto road. There are some stone cabins, one yet inhabitable and [a] well-constructed concrete swimming pool. Water seeping from the hillside supplies the pool which is partially filled with moss and nourishes a school of small fish.
>
> It is an interesting place to camp and one rarely visited except by an occasional duck hunter or wandering prospector [65].

Famous writer and big game hunter Erle Stanley Gardner visited the Soda Springs site around 1936 to shoot bullfrogs, having been guided there by his good friend, Ken Wilhelm, operator of the service station at Manix on I-15. Although he never mentions the site by name, Gardner (author of the Perry Mason murder mysteries, among other titles) published a description of his hunting expedition there entitled "Desert Madness: Hunting the game of the desert with bow and arrow" in the magazine *Field & Stream* [28]. No description of the site beyond that of a pool filled with bullfrogs was included, but Gardner's tale of reaching the spot over the sand dunes in a 1923 touring car named "Leaping Lena" made it sound quite remote and exotic.

CHAPTER SIX

The Springer Years and Modern Times
1944 to 1993

On September 13, 1944, a visitor arrived at Soda Springs whose plans for the place were the most far-reaching to date. For the next thirty years, Curtis Howe Springer worked to make his vision a reality. Finding the site deserted, he followed what he believed was the correct legal procedure and claimed the land under a mining claim. Shortly thereafter, with help from assorted volunteers, Springer began building his dream at the place he called "Zzyzx Mineral Springs and Health Resort." A description of Soda Springs as it first appeared in 1944 was recorded in April, 1969:

> The first time we ever saw it, this was very interesting. The best way you could describe it would be a mosquito swamp. There were standing portions of ruins of three corners of the old fort, and there is a building which we use now as part of our dining room that the men eat in, referred to as the old jail. It had a dirt floor and the roof was made out of burlap sacks and stocks. That's about all that was there [10].

Considering the contrast between the appearance of the site in 1944 and how it looks today, the scope of Springer's vision comes into greater focus. Construction of Zzyzx Mineral Springs is truly an admirable accomplishment. Many of the buildings in use at Soda Springs today date from these years, including the two-story Castle, the Zycott and Lakefront rooms, the Dining Hall, Library and Lecture Room, the Pool House and, down the road to the south, the diesel generator house, the Goat Farm and subterranean rabbit rooms.

In many cases these structures were built using donated war-surplus materials by out-of-work men from Skid Row re-

Figure 15. Zzyzx in the 1940s when tents were used and the building called "Sunrise" was under construction.

Figure 16. Zzyzx, 1955. Courtesy of the Harold and Lucile Weight Collection.

cruited by Doc Springer and brought to the desert for rehabilitation. Construction began first on the block of sleeping rooms known as Sunrise; the rest were completed by 1955 [17]. The fountain on "Enrico Caruso Island" in the middle of the large northern pond called "Lake Tuendae" was a special project, built for the Springers "by a man named for the famous singer, hence the name of the fountain"[18].

Curtis Springer was born December 2, 1896 in Wheeling, West Virginia, the only child of Mildred Howe Springer and Walter A. Springer, a life insurance salesman. He left school at age 15, after completing the ninth grade; however, he maintained he had received numerous honorary degrees, including medical degrees and an honorary Ph.D. in Philosophy from Mecca College in New Jersey. Self-described as a producer of religious programs, a Methodist minister and a salesman of health foods,

Figure 17. Lake Tuendae, Zzyzx, 1955. Courtesy of the Harold and Lucile Weight Collection.

he began advertising his line of health products over the radio in 1928.

After moving to California in the 1940s, Curtis Springer promoted his products at public lectures, first held at the Angelus Hotel, then later at the Alexandria Hotel at Fifth and Spring Streets in Los Angeles. Touted in newspaper ads as "the most sensational, daring and masterful speaker in America today," he offered "two free lectures each day, 2 p.m. and 8 p.m." with such intriguing titles as "Life and How to Live It" and "Why Men, Women Crack After 40".

One of Springer's first health food products was a substance called "Antediluvian Herb Tea," a botanical laxative described by him as "a blend of herbs, roots and barks with peppermint flavor . . . We have shipped over 4 million packages in 30 years . . ." [60]. Other products available at Zzyzx or through the mail included "Zy-Pac Desert Clays with Pen-O-Derm oils," "NCF" (which stood for Nerve Cell Food), "Mo-Hair" (for curing baldness), "O-M-R" (One Minute Relief for indigestion) and "Hollywood Pep Cocktail," to be sprinkled over foods and "containing concentrated vital food energy." Some of these products were made at Zzyzx in converted school buses which were parked near the facility. The late Jerry Gates, former caretaker at Zzyzx who worked for Springer, helped to make "Zy-Crystals" on the premises. Gates described the formula as 10% salt from Soda Lake and 90% epsom salts.

At its peak of popularity, which extended well into the 1960s, Zzyzx Mineral Springs had accommodations for over 100

Figure 18. The Castle, Zzyzx Mineral Springs, Baker, California. Circa 1950s. Courtesy of the Duffield-Stoll Collection.

guests and many times had no vacancies. Curtis Springer and his wife Helen offered their guests a unique blend of health treatments, diet, religion and relaxation in the desert climate. Many found the combination highly attractive and returned many times to enjoy it. Others maintained they found relief for their ailments at Zzyzx where conventional medicine had failed them. A number of former guests have taken the public tours available at the site today and shared their fond memories of earlier visits. Fees for staying at Zzyzx were to be considered donations: "We will accept you with or without money . . . Money is not necessary, though of course, we do expect those whom God has blessed with an income to pay their way at Zzyzx as well as elsewhere". This open-handed generosity also contributed much to the Springers' popularity.

By all accounts the late Curtis H. Springer was an extraordinary person with tremendous personal charisma. He was a large, robust man, over six feet tall with bright blue eyes and a full head of hair, pure white in later years. He drove a large Cadillac convertible and reputedly always carried a big roll of folding money in his pocket. There was a larger-than-life Hollywood quality to him which he cultivated in his persona as radio evangelist. His optimistic, homespun message was set off by interludes of recorded country-western music performed by such favorites as The Sons of the Pioneers.

Springer's radio broadcasts, many recorded in the small room off the library for broadcast below the border, helped spread the fame of Zzyzx Mineral Springs far and wide. In an issue of his newsletter called The Elucidator from 1955, Springer, who called himself "Radio's Friend of Millions" informed his

Figure 19. Photography by Dennis Casebier of the Zzyzx Mineral Springs Sign near the Zzyzx Offramp, I-15, December 1981. Courtesy of Dennis Casebier, Goffs School House.

readers that "we are on the air twice each night, six nights a week over the big fifty-thousand watt XERB, which is located at 1090 on your dial, just between KNX and KXLA." From tapes of his show and his literature, a short list of sayings gives a taste of his philosophy:

> "Be internally, externally and eternally clean."
>
> "God will provide. If you play the game fair, I believe the Big Boss Upstairs will level things out. That's my religion."
>
> "Our God Whom We Serve Is Able."
>
> "Never do anything that you would be ashamed of if your mother saw you, or if the Lord saw you."

What went wrong for Curtis Springer? How can it have happened that on April 11, 1974, after some 30 years of residence, the Springers were bodily evicted from Zzyzx? The answers are there, but it may take some time before they can be viewed in their proper historic perspective.

What is clear is that by the late 1960s, complaints and accusations began to pile up concerning the Springers. Truly sick people arrived at Zzyzx, only to find they were many miles from licensed medical care or even ambulance service. The AMA called him the "King of Quacks," the IRS accused him of tax evasion, the Pure Food and Drug Administration said he was guilty of false advertising, the postal service, various county offices

Figure 20. An ad formerly used announcing Curtis Springer's Radio Programs.

and others were also after him, but the most telling blow was dealt by the Bureau of Land Management (BLM), which disputed his mining claims and eventually led the charge in court. In 1968, BLM initiated legal action against the Springers to evict them from the land and in 1974, after lengthy court proceedings, BLM won its case and took possession of the facilities from the Springers. Curtis and Helen, vowing to fight on, moved to Las Vegas. After a slow decline, Curtis Springer died in December, 1985 at the age of 89.

We gain insight into Springer's complex personality from a report developed by the San Bernardino County probation office after Springer's arrest in 1968.

> Based on the defendant's assertion and agency reports, Curtis Springer is either the most saintly, misunderstood person in the land, or a salesman of unequaled ability. Mr. Springer can justify vocally the fact that he possesses an ardent desire to be of benefit to mankind, that his life is and has been dedicated to bringing happiness and contentment through good health to the many afflicted and aged of our society. His condition of living reflects not that of a person who has realized vast financial gain over the past years, but rather one of frugality. His single-handed accomplishments must be admired. Zzyzx, without splendor, is an enviable achievement for one person to attain.
>
> And, as he admits, it is quite possible that Curtis Springer has been involved for so many years in merchandising through radio advertisements that he has lost track of reality and is selling for the sake of selling. Perhaps he has, in fact, violated laws unknowingly. It is possible that his way of life has become a game with him and he is not fully aware of the dire consequences his buyers must pay because of a misplaced confidence in his title as doctor or in the claims of his products, or the penalty he must inevitably face through the Court of Law because of his inability to conform to that law. [Adult Fact Sheet, San Bernardino County Probation Dept., Case No. 17149-S, October 27, 1969].

Only time will tell the whole story.

Modern Times

In 1976, the BLM signed a five-year cooperative management agreement with the California Desert Studies Consortium, a program of the California State University. The Consortium established the operating structure of the teaching and research facility that now occupies Soda Springs and has renamed it the Desert Studies Center. In 1981, that agreement with BLM was extended by 25 years. Since 1976 changes and improvements have been made at Soda Springs and students and visitors from all over the world have enjoyed the accommodations.

In keeping with the pattern of the past, there are bold visions for the future at Soda Springs. The landscape will con-

Figure 21. Vicki Lane Hill's rendition of the Springer's Goat Farm at Zzyzx Mineral Springs.

tinue to be molded to suit human needs. However, as stewards of the public domain, concern for the water must remain foremost in the plans, as this is the essential link between past, present and future.

Bibliography

1. Academic American Encyclopedia
   1992 Colliers, publisher. Computer access through Prodigy network.

2. Beattie, George W.
   1955 "Preliminary Report of the Archaeological Survey of the Deep Creek Site on the Upper Mojave River" in SBCMA *Quarterly II:2* Winter, published by the San Bernardino County Museum Association, Redlands, California.

3. Belden, L. Burr
   1953 "T & T Built to Tap Death Valley Borate Deposits" in *History in the Making* column, San Bernardino *Sun-Telegram*, Feb. 1, 1953.

4. ———
   1956 "Old Map Reveals Trails, Roads of Fifty Years Ago" *History in the Making* column, San Bernardino *Sun-Telegram*, Aug. 5, 1956.

5. Brooks, George R., editor
   1977 *The Southwest Expedition of Jedediah S. Smith, His Personal Account of the Journey to California, 1826–1827.* A. H. Clark Publishers, Glendale, CA.

6. Cameron, Constance
   1982 *The West Pond Report:* Archaeological Investigations at SBr-363c, Soda Springs (Zzyzx) California. Museum of Anthropology, California State University, Fullerton.

7. Campbell, Elizabth W. Crozer, William H. Campbell, Ernst
   1937 Antevs, Charles Avery Amsden, Joseph A. Barbieri and Francis D. Bode. "The Archeology of Pleistocene lake Mohave: A Symposium" in *Southwest Museum Papers Number Eleven,* published by the Southwest Museum, Highland Park, Los Angeles, Calif.

8. Carder, Thelma.
    1976 "Francisco Garcés, a True Bicentennial Hero for the
    Southwest" in *Once Upon A Desert:* Heritage of People,
    Places and Events. Patricia J. Keeling, editor. A Bicen-
    tennial Project. The Mojave River Valley Museum Asso-
    ciation, Barstow, California.

9. Carter, George F.
    1980 *Earlier than You Think,* A Personal View of Man in
    America. Texas A&M University Press, College Station.

10. Casebier, Dennis G.
    n.d. "Notes" from the files of Dennis G. Casebier; the journals
    of Edward Carlson and Alonzo E. Davis and the testimony of
    Helen Springer, 1969.

11. ———
    n.d. Notes" obtained in 1982 with the heading of "Appendix D",
    "The following chronology highlights significant events im-
    portant to an understanding of Soda Springs", source un-
    known.

12. ———
    1972 *Carleton's Pah-Ute Campaign,* Tales of the Mojave
    Road Number One, June 1972. Casebier, Norco, Cali-
    fornia.

13. ———
    1973 *Camp Rock Spring, California,* Tales of the Mojave
    Road Number Three, Jan. 1973. Tales of the Mojave
    Road Publishing Company, Norco, California.

14. ———
    1975 *The Mojave Road,* Tales of the Mojave Road Number
    Five, Sept. 1975. Tales of the Mojave Road Publishing
    Company, Norco, California

15. ———
    1976 *The Mojave Road In Newspapers,* Tales of the Mojave
    Road Number Six, Jan. 1976. Tales of the Mojave Road
    Publishing Company, Norco, California.

16. Casebier, Dennis G. and Friends of the Mojave Road
    1983 *Guide to the Mojave Road,* Tales of the Mojave Road
    Number 9, October 1983. Tales of the Mojave Road Pub-
    lishing Company, Norco, California.

17. ———
    1986 *Mojave Road Guide,* Tales of the Mojave Road Number
    11, June 1986. Tales of the Mojave Road Publishing
    Company, Norco, California.

18.   ———
       1989   *Guide to the East Mojave Heritage Trail:* Rocky Ridge
              to Fenner, Tales of the Mojave Road Number 15, Octo-
              ber. 1989. Tales of the Mojave Road Publishing Com-
              pany, Norco, California.

19.   Coues, Elliot, Editor
       1900   *On the Trail of a Spanish Pioneer,* The Diary and Itin-
              erary of Francisco Garcés . . . 1775–1776. 2 vols. Fran-
              cis P. Harper, New York.

20.   Drover, Christopher Elvis
       1979   *The Late Prehistoric Human Ecology of the Northern
              Mohave Sink, San Bernardino County, California.* Phd
              dissertation on file at UC Riverside.

21.   Duffield, Anne Q., Rob Fulton and Steven G. Wells
       1990   *Cima Volcanic Field Area,* Road Log and Background
              Information, Appendix III. Desert Studies Center.

22.   Dunn, H.H.
       1930   "Tracing the Pueblos to the Pacific" in *Touring Topics*
              magazine, October, 1930.

23.   Eargle, Dolan H., Jr.
       1986   *The Earth Is Our Mother:* A Guide to the Indians of Cal-
              ifornia, Their Locales and Historic Sites. Trees Com-
              pany Press, San Francisco, California.

24.   Englehardt, Zephyrin
       1927   *San Gabriel Mission and the Beginnings of Los Ange-
              les.* San Gabriel, California.

25.   Flint, Timothy, editor
       1962   *The Personal Narrative of James O. Pattie.* J.B. Lip-
              pincott Company, Philadelphia and New York.

26.   Forbes, Jack D.
       1965   *Warriors of the Colorado.* University of Oklahoma
              Press, Norman, Oklahoma.

27.   Frickstad, Walter
       1955   *A Century of California Post Offices:* 1848–1954.
              Oakland, California.

28.   Gardner, Erle Stanley
       1936   "Desert Madness: Hunting the Game of the Desert with
              Bow and Arrow", pages 18–20, 82–84 in *Field & Stream*
              magazine, September, 1936.

29.   Gavin, John, editor
       1972   *Francisco Garcés:* A Record of Travels in Arizona and Cal-
              ifornia, 1775–1776. John Howell Books, San Francisco.

30.   Glennan, William S.
      1974   "The Baker Site (SBr-541)" pgs. 17–35 in the *Quarterly of the Pacific Coast Archaeological Society*, Vol. 10, No. 2, April 1974. Costa Mesa, California.

31.   Hafen, LeRoy R. and Ann W. Hafen
      1954   *The Old Spanish Trail.* The Far West and the Rockies Historical Series, 1820–1875, Vol. I. Arthur H. Clark Company, Glendale, California.

32.   Hart, Herbert
      1965   *Old Forts of the Far West.* Bonanza Books, New York.

33.   Hatheway, Roger G. and Anne Q. Duffield
      1989   *Ward and Silurian Valleys:* Historical Resource Investigations. Prepared under contract to US Ecology, Newport Beach, California.

34.   Hensher, Alan
      1991   *Ghost Towns of the Mojave Desert:* A Concise and Illustrated Guide. California Classics Books, Los Angeles, California.

35.   Jaeger, Edmund C.
      1958   "Life on an Ancient Mojave Playa" in *Desert Magazine*, Feb. 1958, pgs. 24–26. On Desert Trails with a Naturalist—XLVI.

36.   Johnston, Francis J.
      1980   *The Serrano Indians of Southern California.* Malki Museum Press, Morongo Reservation, Banning, California. Revised 1980 edition.

37.   ————
      1987   *The Bradshaw Trail.* Historical Commission Press, Riverside, California. Revised edition.

38.   King, Chester and Dennis G. Casebier
      1981   *Background to Historic and Prehistoric Resources of the East Mojave Desert Region.* Prepared for the Bureau of Land Management California Planning Program, Desert District Office, Riverside, California.

39.   Kroeber, A.L.
      1976   *Handbook of the Indians of California.* Dover reprint of 1925 edition, Dover Publications, Inc. New York.

40.   Mendenhall, Walter C.
      1909   *Some Desert Watering Places* in Southeastern California and Southwestern Nevada. Water Supply Paper 224, USGS, Washington, D.C.

41.   Miller, Ronald Dean and Peggy Jeanne Miller
      1967   *The Chemehuevi Indians of Southern California.* Malki Museum Brochure No. 3, Malki Museum Press, Banning, California.

42.   Mollhausen, Baldwin H.
       1969   *Diary of a Journey from Mississippi to the Coasts of
       the Pacific,* 2 vols. Translated from the German by Mrs.
       Percy Sinnett. Reprinted 1969 edition, New York.

43.   Moratto, Michael J.
       1984   *Caliifornia Archaeology.* Academic Press, Inc. Har-
       court Brace Jovanovich, Publishers.

44.   Morgan, Dale L.
       1953   *Jedediah Smith* And the Opening of the West. Univer-
       sity of Nebraska Press, Lincoln, Nebraska.

45.   Myrick, David F.
       1963   *Railroads of Nevada and Eastern California,* Vol. 2.
       Howell-North Books, Berkeley, California.

46.   Nakamura, Norm
       1966   "The Baker Site: A Non-Projectile Point Assemblage at
       Pleistocene Lake Mojave" in *Papers on the Archaeol-
       ogy of the Mojave Desert* No. 2, Mark Q. Sutton, editor.
       Reprint, Coyote Press, Salinas, California.

47.   Nordhoff, Charles
       1973   *California:* for Health, Pleasure and Residence. A Book
       for Travellers and Settlers. Centennial reprinting, Ten
       Speed Press.

48.   Peirson, Erma
       1970   *The Mojave River and Its Valley.* Western Lands and
       Waters Series IX. The Arthur H. Clark Company, Glen-
       dale, California.

49.   Robinson, W.W.
       1958   *The Story of San Bernardino County.* Pioneer Title In-
       surance Company, San Bernardino, California.

50.   Rogers, Malcolm J.
       1929   "Report of An Archaeological Reconnaissance in the
       Mohave Sink Region" in Museum of Man Publications
       Archaeology, Vol. I No. 1, February, 1929, San Diego,
       California. Ballena Press reprint, Ramona, California.

51.   ——
       1939   "Early Lithic Industries of the Lower Basin of the Col-
       orado River and Adjacent Desert Areas" in *San Diego
       Museum Papers Number 3,* Museum of Man, San Diego,
       California, reprint 1989 edition.

52.   Rumble, Josephine
       n.d.   *History of Old Government Road Across the Mojave
       Desert to the Colorado River* Including the Pre-historic.
       Work Progress Administration, unpublished, copied
       by San Bernardino County Historical Society, San
       Bernardino, California.

53. Rusling, James F.
    1874 *Across America:* or The Great West and the Pacific Coast. Sheldon & Company, New York.

54. Schroth, Adella B., Bruce Jenkins, L.R.V. Joesink Mandeville
    1983 *Bifaces From the Soda Springs Rockshelter.* A paper presented at the Southwestern Anthropological Association Meetings, San Diego, California, March, 1983. On file at Cal. State Fullerton.

55. Semenza, Taffy
    1983 *Technological Analysis of CA-SBr-5193:* Bifaces from a Prehistoric Quarry Workshop in the Mojave Sink, San Bernardino County, California. M.A. thesis on file at the Desert Studies Center.

56. Shin, Charles Howard
    1980 *The Story of the Mine:* As Illustrated by the Great Comstock Lode of Nevada. Vintage Nevada Series, University of Nevada Press, Reno, Nevada.

57. Silliman, B.
    1866 "On Some of the Mining Districts of Arizona near the Rio Colorado, with Remarks on the Climate, etc." in *The American Journal of Science and Arts,* Second Series, Vol.XLI, No. 123, May, 1866. A paper read before the National Academy of Sciences at Washington D.C., Jan. 1866.

58. Smith, Gerald A.
    1977 *The Mojaves:* Historic Indians of San Bernardino County. San Bernardino County Museum Association reprint.

59. Springer, Curtis Howe
    1955 *The Elucidator,* newsletter from Zzyzx Mineral Springs. Several issues in the Desert Studies Consortium files.

60. Sullivan, Maurice G.
    1934 *Travels of Jedediah Smith.* Fine Arts Press, Santa Ana, California.

61. Thompson, David G.
    1921 *Routes to Desert Watering Places in the Mohave Desert Region, California.* Water Supply Paper 490-B, U.S. Dept. of the Interior, U.S. Geological Survey, Washington, D.C..

62. ———
    1929 *The Mohave Desert Region, California:* A Geographic, Geologic, and Hydrologic Reconnaissance. Geological Survey Water-Supply Paper 578. U.S. Dept. of the Interior, U.S. Geological Survey, Washington, D.C.

63. Udell, John
    1946 *Journal* Kept During a Trip Across the Plains Containing An Account of the Massacre of a portion of His Party

by the Mojave Indians in 1859 [1858]. Kovach, Los Angeles, Calif.

64.   Van Dyke, Dix
      1927   "A Modern Interpretation of the Garces Route" in *Journal of the Historical Society of Southern California*, part IV, Vol. XIII, pgs. 353–359.

65.   ———
      1940   "Old Time Army Fort Found Near Baker" in Barstow *Printer*, Vol. III, No. 5, "No. 24 of a series of fascinating travelogs through the Golden Mojave Empire", September, 1940.

66.   Ver Planck, William E.
      1958   *Salt in California* in Bulletin 175, State Dept. of Natural Resources, Division of Mines, San Francisco, California.

67.   Vredenburgh, Larry M., Gary L. Shumway, Russell D. Hartill
      1981   *Desert Fever:* An Overview of Mining in the California Desert. Living West Press, Canoga Park, California.

68.   Waitman, Dr. Leonard B.
      n.d.   *Raids, Raiders, Law Enforcers and Watch Dogs.* Self-published. San Bernardino County.

69.   ———
      1968   "Horse Soldier Forts of the Mojave Desert" in San Bernardino County Museum Association *Quarterly* Vol. XV, No. 3, Bloomington, California.

70.   Walker, Clifford J.
      1986   *Back Door to California:* The Story of the Mojave River Trail. Mojave River Valley Museum Association, Barstow, California.

71.   Warren, C. N., and H. T. Ore
      1978   "Approach and Process of Dating Lake Mojave Artifacts" in *The Journal of California Anthropology* Vol. 5 No. 2, pgs. 179–187.

72.   Warren, Elizabeth von Till
      1974   *Armijo's Trace Revisited:* A New Interpretation of the Impact of the Antonio Armijo Route of 1829–1830 on the Development of the Old Spanish Trail. Master's thesis in History, University of Nevada, Las Vegas.

73.   Warren, E. von Till, R.H. Crabtree, C.N. Warren, M. Knack, and R. McCarty
      1980   *A Cultural Resources Overview of the Colorado Desert Planning Units.* Riverside: Report to the U.S. Bureau of Land Management.

74.   Whipple, Lieutenant A. W.
      1856   *Report of Explorations For a Railway Route, Near the Thirty-Fifth Parallel of North Latitude, from the Mis-*

sissippi River to the Pacific Ocean. Corps of Topographical Engineers, Assisted by Lieutenant J. C. Ives. Washington D. C.

75.   Williamson, Lieutenant R. S.
       1853 *Explorations and Surveys For a Railroad Route From the Mississippi to the Pacific Ocean:* Report of Explorations in California for Railroad Routes, to Connect with the Routes Near the 35th and 32d Parallels of North Latitude, Corps of Topographical Engineers. War Department, Washington D. C.

Archives Consulted

Dennis Casebier Collection
Duffield-Stoll Collection
Arda Haenzel Collection
Germaine Moon-Mojave River Valley Museum Collection
Hugh Tolford Collection
Desert Studies Consortium Collection
San Bernardino County Public Records

Archaeology at Zzyzx and Environs

Archaeological research at Soda Springs and in the vicinity, begun over half a century ago, has confirmed that prehistoric people knew the area well.

The first archaeologist to report finding the traces of early people on the ancient beach near Soda Springs was Elizabeth Crozer Campbell, who surveyed the area with her husband William in 1934 and 1935[7]. The flaked-stone artifacts found by the Campbells along the ancient terraces around Lake Mojave were considered distinctive by all. Archaeologists now believe they represent the work of previously unknown people dubbed "the Lake Mojave Culture."

In addition to large spear-points, knives, keeled scrapers, choppers, drills, gravers, cores amd hammerstones, the Campbells also found puzzling crescent-shaped stones or "crescentics", whose function can only be guessed. Subsequently, similar Lake Mojave "tool-kits" have been reported from other ancient lakeshores in the Great Basin. These finds tie the Lake Mojave culture to the Western Pluvial Lakes Tradition, at its peak around 10,000 years ago (Warren in 43).

Working sometimes alone and sometimes with assistance, the Campbells surveyed the shoreline of Pleistocene Lake Mojave, collecting as they went. Referring to Limestone Hill at Soda Springs, Elizabeth wrote "down by Soda Hill enough specimens were found to fill two or three cigar boxes . . . The terraces, several hundred yards in width, lying between the Soda Lake Mountains and the limestone hill at the edge of the playa, produced many artifacts and flint chips" [7]. The current whereabouts of these artifacts is not known for certain. Recent (1989–1992) catalog work done by Park Service archaeologists of the Campbell materials at Joshua Tree National

Monument headquarters in Twenty-Nine Palms may provide some clues.

Elizabeth Campbell was clearly not much impressed by Soda Springs as she saw it in 1935–1936.

> Along the eastern base of the rock hills at Soda Station springs flow out on the ground in several places and support a considerable growth of salt grass and tules. We searched well for archaeological remains that might be associated with these flowing springs. No manos or metates were found, no arrowpoints or anything representing modern Indians. The springs are salty and the place is a low unprotected hole at best [7].

Although the Campbells did not succeed in finding the recent remains they sought, other researchers have had better luck. The first of these was Malcolm J. Rogers, an archaeologist working for the San Diego Musuem of Man from the 1920s through the 1940s. With *terra incognita* before him, Rogers focused his efforts on understanding the most numerous remains he found, those which represented the last two thousand years of human use of the desert, as opposed to searching with a mindset for the early material, as the Campbells had.

On his first surveys in the Mojave between 1926 and 1928, Rogers recorded many extraordinary finds near Soda Lake, including stone tools and flakes, decorated pottery, shell beads and even cremated human remains, all within a twenty-five mile radius of Soda Springs [50]. Approximately 10 miles southwest of Soda Springs, at a place he called Mesquite Springs, Rogers found petroglyphs along with artifacts which he labeled Puebloan or "Basket-Maker" in type. In using this terminology, Rogers was following the archaeological tradition of the Southwest, still the dominant force in California museum circles (Notes, "M" Series, Museum of Man Archives, San Diego). With several assistants, he also collected surface artifacts along the shores of Silver Lake, north of Baker [9].

In 1929, Rogers reported having found artifactual evidence of "a scattered but permanent Puebloan population" at nearby Halloran Springs [22] and in the Cronese Lakes region, northwest of Afton Canyon [50]. Based in large part on his analysis of the ceramics, he dated his discoveries to Amargosa II/Basket-Maker III times, around A.D. 700 [51]. Like Elizabeth Campbell, Malcolm Rogers had an agenda; he was looking for evidence of Southwest-type desert agriculture.

> The two Cronise Lakes, situated just west of where the Mohave River enters the Mohave Sink, and into which the

river sometimes empties, have had water in historic times; both are completely surrounded by Indian camps and villages . . .

If agriculture, such as corn culture, was ever practiced in the Mohave Desert, this locus has always seemed to me to have offered the most favorable environment . . . The only evidence that we could find indicative that corn was grown here is the great number of metates and manos present. It is well known that mesquite beans were pounded green in mortars, which are also present, and there is no seed native to the region necessitating the presence of so many large metates [50].

From this first rather conjectural work, Rogers expanded and improved his chronology. In 1939, the Museum of Man published his definitive opus [51]. Well-illustrated and concisely written, it was and still is a landmark study, required reading for modern researchers. Claude Warren, modern successor to these pioneer archaeologists in the East Mojave, aptly summarizes their significance.

These early archaeologists' published reports of the California deserts included elements based on speculation and unstated hypothesis, which led later researchers to question their interpretations. Rogers' 1939 chronology was not wholly accepted by later archaeologists, but it became a theoretical model against which later archaeologists tested their own ideas [43].

Serious archaeological research in the East Mojave was essentially suspended through the 1940s and early 1950s. In the 1960s, when researchers from the UCLA Archaeological Survey turned their attention to the Soda Springs area, the focus of their efforts was the Baker Site (CA-SBr-541).

Located near the town of that name and one and a half miles west of the ancient shoreline of Lake Mojave, an extensive lithic scatter was studied before being obliterated by the widening of Interstate 15. After initial investigations in 1964 by Norm Nakamura and Gene Sterud [46], William Glennan from UCLA completed an analysis of the site in 1970. The Baker Site yielded over 1600 percussion-flaked stone artifacts of which 202 were considered finished or almost finished tools, with all material found at or just below the surface.

This analysis of the artifacts did not give Glennan much confidence in discussing the age of the deposit, though clearly it seemed old to him. He wrote, "The question of the cultural connections and temporal placement of the Baker site are very much open . . . It would appear that the Baker site represents a very early occupation of the Mojave Desert." Further, Glennan believed the site was unique to the area, stating that "a surface survey was made of the western shore area of Pleistocene Lake Mohave in 1969-1970 and no sites producing similar lithic assemblages were found" [30].

Despite this assessment, researchers have continued to survey the borders of ancient Lake Mojave and the nearby sink of the Mojave River and nearly all have reported some discovery. In 1976 Jim Benton of Baker reported finding a small group of ground figures some two miles north of the Zzyzx offramp off I-15. As drawn, one of these figures has a vaguely anthropomorphic shape (Haenszel, personal communication, SBCM 3058 A-D).

Constance Cameron of CSU Fullerton reported that "a large archaeological survey which included Soda Springs was conducted by the University of Nevada Las Vegas Archaeological Research Center in 1978 for the BLM (Bureau of Land Management) and one week of fieldclass work was conducted by CSU Dominguez Hills in 1979" [6]. The results of these surveys have not been published. In August, 1979, Christopher Drover from UC Riverside completed his dissertation study of the Cronise Basin, following Malcolm Rogers' trail [20].

In the fall of 1979, CSU Fullerton Anthropology Department initiated the fieldwork phase of the Lake Mojave Archaeological Project, using the Desert Studies Center as their lab and field camp. Faculty and students conducted an archaeological survey of Pleistocene Lake Mojave shoreline features between Soda Springs and the freeway. For the next three seasons, mapping and recording of trails and artifact scatters was a primary goal. Surveys were also conducted for the first time high in the Soda Mountains where evidence of prehistoric quarrying was encountered at several loci (Cameron, personal communication, 1981).

In April of 1980, CSU Fullerton archaeology students and faculty began excavations at the West Pond, at Soda Springs proper. At the request of the BLM, a series of test units were put in around a small holding pond, with the surprising result that a partially cremated burial feature was exposed. In the fall of 1980, with assistance from students from CSU Los Angeles, excavation units were expanded at the West Pond and testing was completed.

A radiocarbon date for the partially cremated, headless remains found at West Pond was obtained using bone collagen. The results indicated a date of "modern or less than 150 years B.P." (Before Present). This radiocarbon date along with an analysis of the ceramics and projectile points found in association with the burial led to the conclusion that the lady of the West Pond was buried there between A.D. 1600 and A.D. 1850. Her age (adult) and sex were determined by an examination of the bones, and her cultural affiliation (Chemehuevi) was suggested by the grave goods, orientation, etc. [6].

When the research facilities and accommodations at Soda Springs were improved in the early 1980s, two significant archaeological investigations were begun in the immediate vicinity. From 1982 to 1983, Taffy Semenza, a graduate student from CSU Los Angeles, studied prehistoric lithic technology in the Soda Mountains, as represented by artifacts found in a large quarry site on the eastern face behind Soda Springs. A remarkable abundance and variety of material was recovered from the quarry and analyzed by Semenza [55].

Through 1982, and again in 1987, CSU Fullerton faculty and students conducted excavations at the Soda Springs Rockshelter under the direction of Dr. L.R.V. Joesink-Mandeville (DSC Annual Reports). The Soda Springs Rockshelter is located on the east side of Limestone Hill, a shallow overhang near one of the salt seep areas. In March, 1983, a report was prepared by A. Schroth entitled "Bifaces from the Soda Springs Rockshelter". This report presented an analysis of some of the discoveries found subsurface at this site on the east side of Limestone Hill.

Noting that artifact types recovered ranged from Pinto-period dart points to Shoshonean potsherds and shell beads, Schroth concluded that "the artifacts from Soda Springs Rockshelter appear to indicate connections with cultures in all directions and a temporal sequence from 5000 B.C. or 4000 B.C. to proto-historic . . . Isolated finds and the data from the West Pond indicate a long occupation period for Soda Springs as a whole. Thus, it is not too improbable to hypothesize that the area was a favored prehistoric location" [54].

Dr. Mandeville's research at the Desert Studies Center continued through the summer of 1987 with the excavation of "Meighan's Midden," an area of cultural material near the fire ring on the north end of Limestone Hill. Two meter-square units were dug which yielded artifacts from the Protohistoric period (ca. A.D. 1200–1850) [DSC Annual Report 1987]. The Lake Mojave Archaeological Project is in a holding pattern at present, as is most archaeological research in the Mojave Desert. The resources are still there, however; hopefully this will remain the case until research is resumed.

APPENDIX TWO

Cultural Sequence Chart

The chart on the following page summarizes the sequence of cultural changes that occurred in the East Mojave [43] and is based on observed changes in projectile points recovered from archaeological sites in the area. Projectile point types are used in creating cultural sequence charts because stone tools are readily available and have been exhaustively studied, unlike less common artifacts in the East Mojave, such as pottery sherds. The assumption is that tool changes reflect other changes in the habits and customs of the tool makers.

The locations at which the prehistoric tools were found such as Lake Mojave and Saratoga Springs, have given their names to the cultural divisions, for lack of any better naming method. The left column represents years, beginning with 10,000 B.C., a relatively arbitrary figure. The Death Valley units on the right show the correlation or correspondence between the well-studied cultural sequence known for that valley and that of the East Mojave.

This chart is useful mainly for gaining one's temporal bearings, so to speak, as it was painted with a very broad brush. It shows the sequence of prehistoric occupation of the Mojave Desert with the millenia rounded off for convenience and without indicating any gaps which may have existed. It is certainly subject to finetuning and revision by future archaeological study.

CULTURAL SEQUENCE FOR
THE CALIFORNIA DESERTS

(After Warren, et al, 1980 and Warren in Moratto 1984)

Age in Years	East Mojave Cultural Division	Death Valley Cultural Divisions
B.C. 10000	**Fluted Point Tradition** Clovis-like and Folsom-like points	
9000	**Lake Mojave** (9000–5000 B.C.) Lake Mojave and	Death Valley I
6000	Silver Lake points	
5000	**Pinto** (5000–2000 B.C.) Pinto and Little	Early D.V. II
3000	Lake points	
2000	**Gypsum** (2000 B.C.–500 A.D.)	Death Valley II
1000	Gypsum and Elko points	
A.D. 500	**Saratoga Springs** (500–1200 A.D.) Rose Spring and	Death Valley III
1000	Eastgate points	
A.D. 1200	**Shoshonean–Protohistoric** (1200–1850 A.D.) Desert Side-Notched and Cottonwood points	Death Valley IV
A.D. 1776	**Contact Period** (1776–1900 A.D.) Fr. Garces enters desert, reservation system	